THRIVING AS A COUNSELOR

THOMAS WINTERMAN LMHC

ISBN: 0692878742
ISBN 13: 9780692878743

TABLE OF CONTENTS

Introduction

Being a Successful Counselor

Counseling is an incredible profession. There are very few other vocations that offer such an ongoing opportunity to truly make a difference in the lives of others. Through the process of therapy, you have the awesome privilege and terrifying responsibility of joining with another person to help them overcome some of their greatest obstacles. There are few feelings in this world that can match the pure joy of seeing a client become everything they want to be, but every situation is not like that. There are also few feelings that can match the self-doubt and overall frustration that comes with watching someone willfully and purposefully self-destruct, then shrug their shoulders about it and blame you. If you are counseling people you are likely getting paid regardless of the outcome, so are you successful as a counselor no matter what your clients do? That's a great question and one that needs to be addressed early on in this book. What counts as success for a counselor?

Measuring success can very difficult as a counselor, or any helping professional for that matter. Why? Because success is an abstract concept, and one that is easy to define in an area such as business. It's about numbers, and numbers don't lie. The ratio between money coming in and money going out is the definition of success in business. Counseling is not constructed that way. The whole concept of success in therapy is subjective. Insurance companies try to make it less subjective by requiring treatment plans with measurable objectives, such as the frequency and intensity of client symptoms (crying spells, anger outbursts, depressive thoughts, etc.). I understand why treatment plans are required and appreciate the purpose they serve, but using this measure bothers me and here is why. If you measure your success as a therapist by whether or not a client "gets better," you will think you are the worst person in the world — the absolute worst. Why is that? After all, shouldn't therapists be skilled enough to help people get better? Yes, they should, but that data set alone is not reliable. The problem is that there are an endless number of variables when it comes to client symptoms — with the most important and telling variable being whether the client is committed to getting "better." The greatest therapist in the world cannot help a person who is not committed to improvement. Likewise, the worst therapist in the world will be able to help a highly committed client. Oh, and here is another variable: Some client symptoms get worse before they get better. That is just part of the process. Do you understand how maddening this is? If you measure your success by whether a client gets "better," you will burn out in a glorious explosion of expletives and resignation letters. So, what are counselors and other helping professionals to do? How do we measure success? The answer is to challenge the very definition of the word.

One day while working at a nonprofit organization I was approached by a supervisor to speak before the members of the board during a board meeting. The board wanted to know more about what the counseling program did and I was encouraged to share about some successes in my work and the work of my co-workers. I was very excited to have the opportunity to share, and then very sad - I couldn't think of a success. Yikes. I'd been in the field for a number of years and there was not one success story that jumped to my brain as a go-to. There had been many great things that happened and many fulfilling/enriching experiences for me and my clients, but nothing that screamed "success!" I knew what my supervisor wanted; they wanted a story that would wow the board and inspire them to give more money/resources to our program. I was stuck. I didn't want to let my supervisor and co-workers down, but I couldn't stand there and lie. I spent the next several days considering the different approaches I could take to my presentation, and then I came across a quote the day before I was scheduled to present (Side note: I always feel really smart when I say "I came across a quote" as if I spend my spare time reading poetry and examining great speeches. The truth is, just between you and me, I came across this quote because someone on ESPN Radio said it … but no one else has to know that.) Winston Churchill famously said, "Success consists of moving from failure to failure without loss of enthusiasm."

That's it! I knew when I heard it that this was what I was looking for … this is success as a therapist. "Success consists of moving from failure to failure without loss of enthusiasm." I presented on the everyday realities of being a community mental health counselor for a low socioeconomic population at a nonprofit agency. I shared about the daily struggle to get out of bed because some days I didn't know if I was making a difference. I shared that sometimes the only success I could glean from a counseling session was the smile on a child's face because I showed up, or the parent whom I was able to make feel a little better by sitting with them for an hour. I did not have any "wow" type success stories to share and I wasn't ashamed. "Success consists of moving from failure to failure without loss of enthusiasm". (Disclaimer: This does not mean that if you happily suck at your job, then you are successful. You still need the skills.) A successful therapist is one who comes into each session confident, competent and present. Be confident in your training and abilities, be competent with the symptomology you are treating, and be present in body, mind and spirit. Dive in completely, give yourself to your client for that hour (enthusiastically), incorporate the skills, and you will never fail.

Counseling is a profession that is far more difficult than I ever imagined. The paperwork, the bureaucracy, the insurance companies, the co-workers, the clients, their parents and family members, the "system," the courts, the schools, the supervisors, and the politics are all factors that can make this job hard. These factors can either be helpful or harmful, and on bad days it seems that they all stand against me. But my greatest enemy as a therapist? Myself. All of that other stuff can be soul sucking and it certainly contributes to the high burnout rate in the profession, but I am the greatest enemy of my success. My self-doubt, my constant questioning, my never-ending quest for "magical" counseling skills that will completely heal all of my clients — all of it can contribute to a feeling of professional hopelessness and helplessness.

Counseling isn't magic, but it does require considerable skill and expertise, much of which comes with experience and education. For example, when I was in graduate school, Carl Rogers never resonated with me much (we'll talk about him later). I always, being analytical, thought that his person-centered theory of counseling was a little simplistic and, well, naive. Rogers famously stated that there are three conditions (brought to the session by the therapist) that are necessary for client change. The more I practice, the more I realize that his core three predictors for change hold true: empathy, unconditional positive regard, and congruence (congruence signifies realness or genuineness). All the counseling "skills" in the world are useless if you do not bring these three traits into every single session. Are other counseling skills necessary? YES, YES and YES. Again, this is not an excuse to be bad at your job and be happy about it. This is, however, a wake-up call and a challenge to change your perception of success. Let go of your self-doubt and preconceived notions about how to "fix" people. Fix yourself first and your clients will follow.

You might be thinking that success as a counselor is a topic later on in a book like this, but there's a reason I put this topic here. This concept, this idea of challenging how you see success, is something you *have* to carry with you at all times. If you don't, you run a high risk of burn out. Every profession has its challenges and its stresses, but most of them have moments of triumph. You don't really get that as a counselor. Although there will be countless times that you have a positive impact on someone, that impact may not shine through for years. There are many times that your clients will get worse or you will not help at all, but it won't be your fault. You have to go in with the mindset that "success" as a counselor is a self-measurement and is not provided by clients. Move from failure without losing your enthusiasm, and you will have succeeded.

How to use this book/my purpose for writing it
Why did I write this book? To make money, of course! Just kidding. Kind of. I never cared for school much when I was in high school or even into college. School was just bleh to me; something I had to do. When I hit graduate

school, I was shocked - I started liking school. I couldn't wait to go to class, I actually read my textbooks *gasp*, and I would ask questions and actively participate during class. I wanted to soak in every little tidbit of knowledge I could get from my professors. Then I hit what almost every invested graduate student runs into - overload! There was so much information being thrown at me constantly, and it wasn't just boring, run of the mill stuff - these were useful tools I would need down the road. Some semesters felt like I was being hit by a tidal wave of information while standing with a child's sand bucket to capture as much as I could; it felt impossible. I could not soak up every bit of wisdom and remember everything that was thrown at me. I started jotting down and committing to memory the things that seemed most important. I didn't catch everything because it would be impossible, but I tried to get the stuff that mattered most. I would make special notes, record myself talking about the class on my cell phone (that was a little weird), and do whatever I could to hold on to that precious information before it sunk into the obscurity of everything else. That's what is in this book - the major stuff. I wanted to give graduate students, bachelor's level students, practicing professionals, and people interested in the field a guide that hit the highlights. This book does not have everything you need to be a counselor (that takes years of school) but it can be a great tool. It is designed to be read front to back, but also has different chapters ear-marked so you can return to them any time you need to freshen up your memory on a particular topic. Some of the information is textbook-like in that it is factual, and some of the information is the field as I see it. I sincerely hope you can find parts of this book that are of help to you one way or another. After all, that's why I wrote the thing - to help!

PART I

THE NUTS AND BOLTS

CHAPTER 1

THE EDUCATION

Most of the information I am about to give you varies from state to state, and may even change year to year. If you want to be a counselor (and actually call yourself a counselor) then you need a degree from a college. Preferably a master's degree from an accredited college, but more on that later. Some places will hire bachelor's level counselors, but that is usually at a substantially lower pay rate than master's level counselors.

Master's level counselors are quite employable (in my experience), but nearly all the jobs involve providing counseling at local mental health agencies. "Great!" you might think, "Counseling is exactly what I want to do with my counseling degree anyways!" Working in an agency is a great place to get your feet wet and refine your skills, but there are unique challenges that come with this type of work. In many cases the counseling programs are either grant funded or self-sustaining. Grant funded programs receive X number of dollars, typically from the government, to provide a certain service for X amount of years. There are benefits to working with grant funding, including the fact that you know the money will be there for a set amount of time. The scary thing about working with grants is that when the grant expires you may no longer have a job. It could be that the grant is renewed, but there are few guarantees when working with government money.

Self-sustaining programs must bill insurance companies in order to pay their counselors. Billing insurance (in Florida, in 2017) requires that you have a professional license. That license is what assures insurance companies that you are qualified to provide the services they are reimbursing. In a community mental health agency, there are usually a few people who have licenses (typically they are supervisors) and the unlicensed master's/bachelor's level counselors provide services "under" that person's license number. Providing mental health services in an agency setting can be difficult. Many of the clients you will work with have a lot of needs. The clients I served came from a low socioeconomic status, came from broken homes, were removed from their parent's care (or had their children removed), were homeless, jobless, had family issues with substance abuse, and/or had intellectual/functioning troubles. All of these factors made being a mental health counselor tremendously difficult. There were so many issues affecting these people that it was hard, if not impossible, to really and truly help them. As a mental health counselor for a population like this, you will face burnout...quickly. Agency work is not all horror stories though. It is a great place to get experience, work with a wide variety of issues, and make connections with others from many different professions. You will learn the ins and outs of your community, as well as how to help people from all walks of life. The clients served in agency work are not hopeless and they are certainly not unreachable. The work can be rewarding as you will find many victories working at an agency, but the days are long and the pay is low.

Back in the day (I just like saying that) you didn't need any credentials to practice counseling, and in some states you still don't (depending on the wording you use to describe what you do). Life coaching, for instance, is currently an unregulated field. That means I could walk outside right now, declare myself a life coach, and start charging people for those services. The field of life coaching is growing and looks to be moving toward regulation, but that's not the case as of today. But keep in mind, because it is not regulated, insurance companies don't typically pay for life coaching. That means if you want to make a living doing that sort of work you will have to accept only self-pay clients. That may be a reality for some, but in many areas of the country there aren't a slew of people ready to fork out $100 per week for life coaching. There are a lot of similarities between being a life coach and a counselor, but the biggest difference is that a counselor can and does treat disorders. Counselors can do life coaching, but life coaches can't be counselors.

You must have at least a bachelor's degree (four years of college) to practice professional counseling, and in most cases you will need a master's degree (two additional years of college) as well. The gold standard in the counseling field is a license. In Florida, having a license makes you a Licensed Mental Health Counselor (LMHC). In other states, you are a Licensed Professional Counselor (LPC). A license allows you to bill private insurance for your services and gives you the flexibility if you wish to go into private practice. If you want to become licensed as a counselor, that is regulated through your state. To be an LMHC in Florida you must start with a master's degree from an accredited college. If you don't know whether or not a college or program you are considering is accredited, ask them because it is VERY important. A counseling degree from Back Alley University or Rip-Off Tech won't do for licensure. Do some research and make an informed decision. The accrediting body for counseling programs is called the Council for Accreditation of Counseling and Related Educational Programs, or CACREP for short. CACREP goes around and holds counseling programs to high standards, which is good for you because it ensures you meet the needed requirements to move forward with licensure.

As technology continues to advance at such a rapid rate there are more and more colleges and universities offering online counseling degrees. Whether or not the college you attend is online, in person, or a hybrid of both is a matter of personal preference more than anything else. And keep in mind that the program's accreditation is the most important factor. In the early days of online college you could never be sure what sort of education you would be getting, but more and more online programs are becoming accredited and acceptable by meeting the high standards of the accrediting body. Personally I don't like online learning, but that is because I learn better in person. I would tend to slack off and not give my full attention to a streaming online lecture, whereas in the classroom I would be more focused. Again, that is just a matter of personal preference.

Licensure

Licensure is typically the highest standard that can be achieved in the profession. A license is your proof that whatever state you live in has given you the okay as a professional. A degree from a college will follow you wherever you go and no one can take it from you, but a license is contingent on your professional standing (and paying your state a bunch of money). If you want to get into the field of counseling my advice is to make licensure your goal. A license is a golden ticket to numerous job opportunities not available to a person who holds a master's or even a PhD. Another bonus is that with a license you can bill insurance companies for providing therapy to clients. You do not have to have a license to practice counseling (in most states), but you would only be able to accept self-pay clients without one. In Florida, you are referred to as a Licensed Mental Health Counselor, but you are also considered a Licensed Practitioner of the Healing Arts, which sounds really cool.

If licensure is your goal (and it probably should be) you need to be prepared to pay a lot of money to get there. And I am not talking about the tens of thousands you already paid for a master's degree. Let's look at the costs (note: all costs are based on 2017 numbers, and they will likely go up). After you have completed your master's degree you must apply to become an intern for your state ($150), then you have to complete two years of post-master's supervision under someone who is approved by the board. Almost all supervisors charge, and a low fee would be $50 per hour; you have to have 100 hours of supervision over two years. At some point during your internship you have to pass the national counselor exam (it's a bear), and the cost for that is $300. There are many folks who have to take this test two, three, or even four times - and you have to pay each time you take it. Also during your internship, you have to complete several trainings to get what is known as Continuing Education Credit (or CEUs) and the cost of pre-licensure CEUs run around $100. And there are several other fees here and fees there that will pop up randomly. What am I telling you? Is it even worth it? Oh yeah, it's worth every penny. I just don't want you to be blindsided by this. This was not something I had personally budgeted for or really prepared for. You need to be thinking about these factors now.

So how is being licensed as a counselor different from other helping professions, such as being licensed as a social worker? That's a great question. Functionally they aren't different at all. In Florida, a Licensed Mental Health Counselor (LMHC) and a Licensed Clinical Social Worker (LCSW) are licensed under the same statute, giving them the exact same privileges as far as the state is concerned. The education requirements and curriculum is a little different for the two programs, and the job outlook is usually better for those who are licensed as social workers. There are typically more employment opportunities for social workers because they work in more settings than counselors. You will find social workers in the military, hospitals, nursing homes, and a variety of places you may not find counselors. I suggest you speak with an academic advisor and do some research to make an informed decision if you are not sure which path you want to take. I received my bachelor's degree in social work, then decided to change course and get my master's in counseling psychology. The biggest reason I changed was that as I was going through my social work studies I realized that counseling was what I wanted to do, and I felt that a counseling degree would be more specific to what I wanted than a social work degree.

A doctorate degree

Once I started in graduate school my thirst and desire for knowledge in my field took off. I wanted to study, know more, and be the best I could be. I was only a couple of classes into my graduate degree when I decided I wanted to earn a doctorate. Why not? I love learning this stuff, I am good at it, and I want to be the best. I was filled with excitement and optimism...until I started doing some research. In case you don't know (because I didn't know), PhD stands for Doctor of Philosophy. And you can imagine, becoming a Doctor of Philosophy in any subject is going to require a lot of research, paper writing, and cash. Education is a big business and you can find (just like a master's degree) a counseling or psychology PhD program that will accept you in a heartbeat after you finish your graduate degree. They all want your money, and as of right now a doctorate (if you already have an accredited master's) will cost you between 30 and 90 thousand dollars. Yes, you read that right. And you need to consider that the best programs will not be entirely online, with many of them are adopting a "hybrid" learning system. That means that many of the courses are available online, but there are also required "intensives" a couple of times per year. An intensive is when you must be on campus for a week or two at a time for classes almost all day every day. Having intensive class sessions can complicate things, because if you have a job you have to take those one to two weeks off, you have to pay for a hotel room, food, etc. This is where you need to start asking some tough questions and doing some math to decide if a doctoral degree is right for you.

In a lot of fields a doctorate automatically equals more pay, but with counseling this is not the case. Sure, you will be more marketable if you plan on working at an agency or in a facility, but you will not earn more money in private practice just because you have the degree. Having a license is what allows you to bill insurance companies for therapy, and having a doctorate degree might allow you to negotiate slightly better fees, but this is not a guarantee. Consider this too: if you want to become licensed as a psychologist instead of a counselor you must have a doctorate degree from a program that is accredited by the American Psychological Association (APA). Being a licensed psychologist allows you to perform certain tasks and bill insurance companies for services that a counselor is not technically qualified to perform. This is a great goal to have, but do your research. APA accredited doctoral degrees are typically mostly offered on location only (few to no online classes), are highly competitive, and have more time requirements.

Another goal for many who seek to get a doctorate degree would be to teach at the graduate level. Graduate level instructors can make great money and have a rewarding job. In order to teach at the graduate level, you must have a doctorate degree of some type in the field you are teaching. To be an adjunct (a part-time teacher) the restrictions are a little loose, but if you want to be become a full-time graduate instructor you will need an accredited doctorate degree. Yeah, it gets confusing and really messy. Make sure you do your research.

A PhD is not the only type of doctorate degree, it's just the most common. There are many areas in counseling and/or psychology you have a doctorate in. You can have an EdD (doctor of education), PsyD (doctor of psychology), and many others. And there are a plethora of areas in which you can have a PhD. Do a quick Google search and you will see what I am talking about. Each degree is different and has its own merits. Research and find one that fits what you want to do and who you want to be.

Okay, so it sounds like I am putting down doctorate degrees, but I am not. If I had the money and time I would do it in a heartbeat. What are some of the good things about a doctorate degree? First off, and maybe most importantly, people will call you doctor. Now that's cool. That's almost worth $50,000 in itself isn't it? There is a certain prestige, clout, and honor that comes with a doctorate degree. You have truly separated yourself from your peers academically. And not only that, but you can separate yourself in marketing a private practice. If I am considering going to a counselor and I see two who are basically the same, except one has a PhD and one has a master's, I'm going with the PhD every time. There is marketing value in a doctorate degree; people automatically have a higher regard for your work. A doctorate degree also gives you more flexibility with jobs down the road. There are many who earn a doctorate degree and work in private practice for a number of years, then transition into teaching at the graduate level. It's a nice way to shift gears later in your career and it is helpful to have that flexibility. And remember, you can't lose an educational degree. What do I mean by that? If you don't renew your license every so often it can be revoked. Or, if you happen into some ethical trouble your license can be stripped. No one can take away a doctorate degree. Once you earn it, that baby is yours.

I did the research and came up with the following: I would love to have a doctorate degree. I know I could do the work and would enjoy the program. However, if I was going to do it I would do it right and get my degree from an accredited institution (means a little higher tuition and tougher coursework). I would likely be paying about $50,000 for my doctorate. I

---

can't pay that out of pocket so I would have to get a loan (yikes). Suddenly my $50,000 degree is $75,000 by the time I pay it off. And what am I getting in return? Well I want to run a private practice so I would not get much more money per client I saw. And on top of that, doing all that school work and traveling to the campus for intensives (one or two week long sessions at the college) would take away from growing my business and, oh yeah, my family. I want to earn a doctorate and I believe I will one day, but today it is just not practical for me.

Specialized Certifications

Apart from degrees awarded by academic institutions you can also earn specialized certifications that make you more competent to treat a specific condition or more effectively utilize certain treatment modalities. Highly specialized types of therapies such as hypnotherapy and sex therapy require specific certifications just to practice. There is a certification available for just about anything to separate you from the crowd if you are looking to practice in a specific area (everyone wants to make a buck). You can become certified as an addiction professional, a play therapist, and just about everything in between. There are also specialized treatment approaches you can be certified in that are useful for treating specific disorders. For example, Dialectical Behavior Therapy (DBT) has been shown to be most effective for treating personality disorders, and Eye Movement Desensitization and Reprocessing (EMDR) is effective in treating trauma, and specifically Post Traumatic Stress Disorder. These are just two examples of many options for certification or specialized training.

Is certification worth it? It depends on what your goals are. If you plan to build your practice by working only with children, a certification in play therapy is something you might want to consider. In most cases certification is not necessary, but it does two things: 1) it gives you specialized knowledge and can truly make you an expert in your specific field, and 2) it's a great marketing tool. If my child needed therapy I would go and see the certified play therapist before seeing the everyday licensed counselor. However, you must consider that these certifications will almost always cost money, and they are not normally cheap. And many times, they require multiple training sessions over several weeks, continuing education, and some of them even require years of practice under the supervision of a qualified supervisor.

CHAPTER 2

THE WORK

Agency Work

This is where most people land when they are fresh out of graduate school. Agencies are almost always hiring (that should be a clue about the work), and the pay is decent. Many agencies not only hire full time counselors, but they also employ people on a contract basis. If you are a contractor that typically means you do not receive a salary, but get paid a set amount for every client hour you bill. Contracting comes with its own set of pros and cons to be considered. The average pay for contract work in my area is about $30 per therapy hour. $30 an hour sounds pretty good, and there is in many cases no cap on that. That means you can see as many people as you want and make as much money as you want. However, your pay is contingent upon you providing therapy. No shows, cancellations, sick days, and vacation days mean you do not get paid. And as a contractor in an agency setting you will either be seeing people in the office or traveling to their home/school. This adds another issue - travel time. You might be reimbursed for mileage, but the time spent driving from one appointment to the other adds up quick. Not only do you have those factors to contend with, but you also do not get paid for completing the necessary paperwork. You have to complete a note for every time you see a client, update treatment plans, renew certifications (for certain insurances), and a slew of other random things. The time really adds up. Also, remember that in many cases contract employees are not offered benefits, and this is a deal breaker for a lot of people. The money is good and you can make a living doing work as an agency counselor, but it can be difficult to manage your schedule.

A huge positive to this type of work is that you get to make your own hours. You are not stuck in an office for 8-10 hours a day, and you can come and go as you please. Most agencies I have worked for do not really care what you do during your days as long as you see your clients and complete your paperwork on time. Does your kid have a doctor's appointment at 9:30? Done. You can move your clients around how you need to in order to get things done you need to get done. That is huge plus. You still have to see all your clients, but you have a lot of flexibility.

The hours are long and the job is hard, but working for an agency can be tremendously rewarding. There are some opportunities for advancement, as all those counselors need a supervisor or supervisors. Putting in your time at an agency, becoming licensed, and working as a supervisor is a great path that many choose to go down. If you are dedicated to an agency and do your job well, they will take care of you.

Inpatient versus outpatient care

Your typical agency work falls into the category of outpatient care, meaning that you see your clients in your office, at their home, or another setting such as school or daycare. Inpatient care involves working in a facility that provides either acute or long-term care. An acute care facility is where individuals go for immediate crisis intervention, often after they have been Baker Acted. These facilities have patients for anywhere from three days to two weeks, depending on the need. Counselors in these settings provide crisis intervention care, individual and group counseling, and work with the other professionals (doctors, nurses, social workers) to provide a plan of care. Long-term facilities are for individuals with chronic conditions who cannot function in society on their own for whatever reason. These facilities often provide daily counseling sessions, whether it be individual or group, and focus on rehabilitation. In most of these facilities (acute care and long-term care) you can be employed with a master's degree, but having a license will make you far more marketable.

Private Practice

Private practice is the golden goose of counseling; it's what most starting out dream of doing. Why? Because you get to set your own hours, be your own boss, and your income ceiling is typically much higher than in an agency or a facility. When I was sitting in my graduate school orientation class of roughly 25 people, at least 15 shared that their goal after school was to work in private practice. As I looked around the room a thought struck me. I live in a mid-size town and these orientation classes are held every year with a brand-new flock of students eager to learn and get started. If about 15 people (the numbers are different every year) start their graduate school experience planning to be in private practice, what will happen to the counseling market? There is no way that our community could support that many private practitioners. Then I had another line of thinking. There are clearly not hundreds of private practitioners in my area, so what happened to those who didn't make it? If that many people dream of going to private practice, and only about 10% or so do, what's the rub? Why are they all not successful? This was a frightening thought to me. Is it luck? Are there secrets I don't know? Are others not willing to put in the work? The answer may be a little bit of all those. As I went through my graduate program and worked in the mental health field I saw many practitioners open their doors, then shut them months later. As I was moving toward licensure and planning on opening a private practice, that really scared me. Not making money was not an option for me.

There are volumes of books and articles on how to be financially successful in private practice, so I am only going to give you a few pointers and basics:

1. Sell yourself - When that wonderful day comes and you open your doors offering to heal the masses with your impressive array of counseling interventions, it won't mean squat if no one shows up

or has never heard of you. As a private practitioner, you are selling yourself and you need people to buy you. It starts in your first graduate class. Work hard, be smart, and impress people. This is the beginning of your referral base. Most of the people who graduate with you will be working in the field in one way or another, and those relationships will be the foundation of your referral base, networking opportunities, and colleagues to bounce ideas off of or collaborate with. Your image - what others think of you - starts now. Put in the work, be a person of integrity, study, and know your stuff. And your marketing doesn't end in graduate school. Your first job out of school in the mental health field will likely be at an agency or other similar facility. Do good work, don't cut corners, and help people. Again, these connections that you make will stick with you. You are building your reputation with everyone you meet. When someone asks what you do proudly share it with them. Don't water it down, be meek, or undervalue yourself. Tell people you are a clinician in the business of helping people (or however you want to phrase it). Because of my personality I tend to undersell myself or make self-deprecating remarks when discussing me, but I am working on that. If I don't buy what I do or who I am, why would anyone else?

2. Have a plan, be prepared - You need to be realistic about this. What is your step by step plan to opening a private practice? Sure, you need a master's degree and license, but what else do you need? You need a business license, a place to practice, furniture, a way to answer the phones, a website, a way to bill insurance companies (if you go that route), a plan for marketing, and the list continues. All this stuff is doable, but you have to plan for it early or it will sneak up on you. Know how much it costs to run a business; make a spreadsheet; do some market research by meeting other private practitioners. They would most likely love to chat with you about what it takes to make this happen. Part of your plan needs to include an understanding of your community and the needs of the people

who live there. If you live in a small rural town the needs of your community will be different than those of a larger city population. Do you live in a military town? Is your town built largely on tourism? Is there another nearby community that your services would be better suited for? These are all questions you need to answer as part of your business plan. Think about it. If there aren't enough people in your town who need the specialized treatment you want to offer, will your business succeed?

3. Get a private practitioner as a mentor and/or supervisor - This is invaluable. Find someone who has walked where you plan to tread and find out how they did it. This is where you can get real life advice and information that you will need to be successful. How much does it cost to operate a counseling practice in your area? How many clients can a practitioner realistically see in a week? How many hours do you need to work to be financially stable? What marketing and networking opportunities are available in your community? A mentor and/or supervisor who is currently practicing in your area will know all of this, and they will likely be happy to share all that and more with you. They can also be your sounding board for ideas and a referral source. Therapists refer clients to therapists they know and trust. Gain some trust amongst your colleagues and you can refer clients to each other who would be a good fit.

4. Find a niche and become an expert - The counseling field is huge. There are so many reasons that people seek out counseling that it is impossible to be an expert in all of them. And people want to see an expert; they want the best. As a private practitioner, the best thing you can do for your business is to be the _____ person. Yes, that blank is there on purpose. What are you passionate about? What areas of counseling are your best? What do you want to learn more about? That's the area you should focus on. Specialize in something. If you were having marriage issues, would you prefer to see a general counseling practitioner who "treats

everything from depression to couples" or would you rather see the person who specializes in couple's therapy? It's the specialist, every single time. If you start to specialize in something, and you become good in this area, word will spread. Practitioners will catch wind of it and they will send clients with this issue to you. Why? Because you are the ____ person, the go-to expert in this area. Some focus on certain age groups - children, adolescents, middle aged, elderly, etc. Some find that certain disorders or common issues can be their specialty - ADHD, depression, anxiety, marital discord, weight loss, PTSD, etc. Whatever it is that interests you, whatever excites you; get in there and become an expert. Go to seminars, take courses online, devote your time to becoming an expert in whatever that is. Do you know how most people find their specialty? They get out of school and start working or interning somewhere. They get some experience under their belt, become competent with a certain population or common issue, and then comes the confidence to work toward being a specialist. My advice is to get out there and work with as many populations and disorders as possible. You will probably find something that makes you excited, something that makes you want to get up in the morning and go to work. When you find it, you will know.

5. Have an income plan - This is one of the most difficult (and sometimes gut-wrenching) parts of the process. How much money do you need to make for this work? Make a list of your potential expenses. If you don't have a clue what those numbers would be, do some research and estimate it. Have a ballpark idea of how much money you need to make, and then break that down. How many clients will you need to see to make that happen? Are you going to quit your full-time job and devote all your time to your practice? Can you do that financially? Many private practitioners have to phase in their private practice while continuing to work full time. This is, for many people, the time that will make or break them.

This is when the going gets tough. You work hard all day, leave your job at four or five, and instead of going home to your family...you go to your other job for several hours. Unfortunately, this is what it takes for many to be successful. You must be willing to sacrifice early to make great gains later. If that is not what you want that's fine, but know that going in. Make a plan for what you need to do to be successful with your finances, and either go for it or make a new plan.

6. Understand that you are a business owner - The rules are different for business owners than they are for people who are employees. I've heard the analogy that owning a business is like having a baby. Sometimes the baby needs to eat when you really want to do something else. Sometimes you have to care for the baby when you don't feel well. Sometimes the baby will take precedent over the rest of your family, your friends, and social life. Owning a business takes sacrifice, but sacrifices early on can pay huge dividends later. As a mental health counselor, you are paid to counsel people, whether that is by private pay or through insurance. You count on people coming to see you weekly. Think about that. Your hours will likely not be 8 AM to 4 PM, Monday through Friday. Many of the people you will see have jobs and cannot make a counseling appointment every Tuesday at 10 AM. This is where you have a choice - you can make sacrifices and grow your business, or you can draw a line in the sand. Your line must be drawn somewhere, after all, you will likely not want to see clients until midnight every night. Every practitioner has a different mindset when it comes to scheduling. And remember this: clients = money. Want to take a sick day? That's money you are not making. Want to go on a two-week vacation? That will cost you two weeks' worth of pay. Health insurance? That comes out of your pocket now. When you are in session you need to think like a clinician, but all other times you need to think like a business owner.

School Counseling - School counseling is an odd profession, and that's something I did not learn until I started doing the work. School counseling is odd because state to state, district to district, and even school to school you will find that the school counselors have varied duties within the school. If you are a counselor for an outpatient facility your job is counseling - you do counseling and you get paid for counseling. As a school counselor (based on my experience as a school counselor and speaking with other school counselors) you become something of a jack of all trades. There are specific roles for school counselors that are seemingly universal (as far as I know). Almost all school counselors seem to be in charge of district/state testing protocols and the overall administration of those tests, which is a bear and almost a full-time job in and of itself. Some school counselors handle discipline issues (investigating situations, calling parents, deciding punishment), some handle more administrative tasks (scheduling meetings, participating in IEP, 504, ESOL, etc. meetings), some handle attendance issues, and on and on. And that's just at the elementary level. Middle and high school level counselors spend a bulk of their time on scheduling and working with students on planning for the future. The truth is that a school counselor can do their job, by the district and school standards, and not provide any counseling to anyone. For a lot of folks that's great. It's part of the reason I wanted to become a school counselor when I moved from the community mental health setting. I like counseling kids, but I also like being left alone. Being a school counselor provided me with ample opportunity for both of those things. I do know this though: most schools are hungry for a mental health expert who can help. If you want to make a difference, are a go-getter, and are creative, the school system is a great place to work. Just know that most of the counseling interventions and ideas you want to implement will likely have to occur after you have completed your other tasks. If you are truly interested in school counseling and you have the credentials, apply for a position and speak with the principal about what the expectations are for the position. Then flip it on them and share your expectations - share what you want to do and what you hope to accomplish. Share with the principal that you want to provide counseling services and how those services will impact and improve test grades. I'm a big fan of Google (if you didn't know that already), so Google some scholarly articles on the effects of _____ on test grades. Target a specific issue (like test anxiety) and describe how you will counsel and help students with anxiety which will improve test scores (based on the data you have), and ultimately will improve the school.

CHAPTER 3

FOLLOW THE CODE

A counselor helps people, plain and simple. However, "helping people" is not a concept that is easily defined. I spoke with an individual (in graduate school) whose idea of helping people was to yell, scream, and berate them. Is that helpful? Maybe for some, but a majority would say no thanks to that type of therapy. There are individuals who need a swift kick in the rear to get motivated to change, but generally speaking this is not a great way to practice counseling. Helping others may sound easy, but it can be tricky. That's because you always have a moving target. What is helpful for one person might not be helpful for another. Helping falls into such a broad range of interventions that it could be argued that you can do whatever you want in the name of "helping". Because of this ambiguity, the profession came up with a code of ethics to provide some boundaries and guidelines for those interventions.

Code of Ethics

For starters, let's talk about a common question with ethics. What is the difference between morals and ethics? They are two words that are very closely related and have similar meanings, but put very simply: morals are personal beliefs and standards while ethics are professional beliefs and standards. Look at almost any group of professionals who do the same type of work and you will likely find an organization representing them that has a code of ethics. What are the ethics of the counseling profession? Autonomy, beneficence, nonmaleficence, fidelity, and justice. I know what you're thinking - those words sound like something the Knights of the Round Table would shout just before battle. These are not just fancy words that sound awesome though; they are the guiding ethical principles for the counseling practice. These words do not constitute the entirety of the Code of Ethics for the counseling profession, but these are the pillars on which the code is built. You can find the entirety of the code here: https://www.counseling.org/resources/aca-code-of-ethics.pdf. Let's talk about what these words mean and what their implications are.

Autonomy: Autonomy basically means freedom. It is the right of a person to govern themselves and make their own decisions. As a mental health professional, this one can be tough sometimes. When a client is making decisions that are contradictory to what you would do, you will often feel an urge to force or maybe just nudge them in the direction you think is right. Don't worry, this is just human nature. Many clients are standing on metaphorical train tracks staring at the pretty light coming straight toward them, and you will feel the urge to push them out of the way. Except you can't. They can decide where they stand and what they do. As long as they are not breaking any laws or are not mentally capacitated in some way, they can do what they want to do. Your job as a counselor is to foster that autonomy and help that person make decisions that are unbiased and based in reality. One situation in which this often comes into play is working with the elderly. At some point a person becomes unable to care for themselves because of their age, and a helping professional wants to do the right thing: they want the elderly individual to go into some sort of managed care setting so they can be provided the care and assistance they need to continue living a full life. There are many elderly individuals who don't want to do this and would prefer to remain in their homes. "But they'll die in their home!" many people would say, including family members. If the person is of a sound mind they cannot be forced to move into a nursing home or any other facility. They have the right to choose what happens. As a counselor, your job is to help the individual understand all their options and come to a decision, not to coerce them into doing what you think they should do.

Beneficence: Beneficence means working for the good of the person you are helping. The well-being of the client in front of you should always be considered when making a decision as a counselor. There are many ways to interpret what a client needs at any given moment, but your decision should include an inner dialogue that asks, "Is this decision the best for my client?" If the answer is yes, and you are not violating any of the other ethical tenets, you are likely making the right choice.

Nonmaleficence: This means "do no harm". At first glance it might appear that beneficence and nonmaleficence mean the same thing, but there is a distinct difference between the two. This difference is especially important when weighing the risk versus the reward of treatment interventions. The best example that comes to mind is paradoxical interventions. This is a fancy way of saying reverse psychology. When using a paradoxical intervention, you would tell a client to, in many cases, intentionally do the thing they are trying to stop doing. Paradoxical interventions are powerful and work wonders with specific clients at specific times. However, an ethical clinician needs to carefully weigh the risk versus the reward. Telling a depressed or anxious client to purposefully feel depressed or anxious could have terrible results, or great rewards. When weighing these decisions, working for the good of your client has to be measured against what might do them harm.

Fidelity: Fidelity is faithfulness, or being trustworthy. Coming to therapy is a huge risk for many people. A lot of individuals feel vulnerable, scared, and come to therapy as a last resort. They must know that they can trust you. The level of trust in the therapeutic relationship will also say a lot about long-term treatment results. The greater the trust level, the greater the odds of the client being successful. Make confidentiality sacred to you, and carefully decide what information to disclose in times where disclosure is a necessity.

Justice: Treat all your clients fairly and equally. Every client you see deserves your very best. They deserve your full attention and entire complement of treatment strategies.

Many times we can get stuck thinking that the Code of Ethics serves as merely a means to catch counselors acting poorly, but the Code of Ethics is there to protect you as a counselor as well as the clients you serve. Being sued or practicing recklessly is something that happens to counseling professionals from time to time. This is a very frightening proposition, and can have disastrous outcomes. One of the ways you can protect yourself as a counselor is to ask yourself if you are following the guiding principles of the code of ethics. When you feel that you are in a gray area and you are not sure what you should do, refer back to the principles. If you do what is right by the client and have strong reasoning for why you acted the way you did, the case against you is weakened. In that way, the code of ethics can protect counselors by providing a standard that can be leaned on when you are not sure how to proceed.

CHAPTER 4

A Few Do's and Dont's

So, what does a counselor do? That is, after all, what this book is about. Instead of taking a broad look at what a counselor does, let's narrow the focus. This information about what counselors do and don't do are very important, but don't carry the strong ethical implications of violating a person's autonomy or purposefully causing harm. Two words you will hear tossed around often in the arena of counseling are "best practice". Best practice basically means what you are supposed to do to be good at counseling, but not doing these things won't land you in ethical trouble. I didn't find out until graduate school that I had a lot of misconceptions about what a counselor is and is not supposed to do (thanks a lot TV), and I found these fascinating.

Counselors Don't Give Advice, But They Do Give Directives
I thought that giving advice was rule number one as a counselor. Nope! I was wrong. Not only is it not rule one, but you shouldn't do too much of it at all. A 'consultant' gives advice, but a counselor does not. This is a difficult lesson to learn as a counselor, and many graduate students (myself included) struggle with this. Counselors do not give advice during a counseling session. Why is this so difficult of a concept to get? Because a lot of people who get into the counseling field already have a lot of experience in helping people. You will hear many counseling students, when asked what led to them being interested

in the field, state, "People have always come to me for help with their problems. I guess I just have that quality about me." This is not necessarily a problem or bad thing, but it has led to a lot of experience in giving advice. So, when you enter a counseling session that is what comes out because it is what you have known and what has worked.

Not giving advice is also difficult because clients oftentimes have a lot of experience in asking others for it. There are many instances in which a client has flat-out asked me, "What should I do?" Yikes. That can put you in a tough spot if you do not know what to say. So why don't counselors give advice? Because counseling is a place for the client to explore their feelings, learn about themselves, and develop their own strategies for making lasting and effective change. So, what should you to a client who asks for advice? The go-to response for counseling students and those new the field is usually, "Have you tried…?" but this is giving advice. Stay away from advice, and guide the conversation toward self-discovery on the part of the client. Your client may say, "What should I do?" and your response could be, "What are your options?" or "What have you tried before?" "Did that work?" "Why or why not?" At this point you are guiding the session toward a solution, but one that the client is coming to on their own.

While counselors don't offer advice (typically) they do give directives, and these directives are often centered around interventions. What does this mean? Directives are, specifically, telling someone to do something. In counseling this often takes the shape of homework. On a personal note, I'm not a fan of using the word "homework" to describe what you are asking clients to do because it often has such a negative connotation attached to it. Yes, I hated homework as a kid and still do. I don't have a better word (yet), but homework always sounds like a bad thing to me. Anyways, giving a directive would be telling your client to journal, take note of every time X happens, take their spouse out for a nice dinner, etc. What is the difference between giving advice and giving a therapeutic, intervention-driven directive? There are several. One difference is that advice often comes from a place of wanting to be right, feel smart, and save the day. Who doesn't want to do that? It's human nature to want to help someone in need, but check yourself for why you are offering up the information. Is it truly for your client, or is it for you? Also, directives are often (and should be) research-based interventions for improving whatever issue the client is facing. For example, journaling has been shown time and time again, through peer reviewed/evidenced-based research, to help people process their feelings and achieve a level of peace. Would asking a client to keep a journal be advice? In a broad sense, maybe. The difference is in the intent, what is asked, and the processing of the intervention that should follow.

Counselors Don't Criticize, But They Do Challenge

Caring about someone and trying your best to help them can be tough. You often go through a phase of wanting to yell, "Why did you do that?! What did you think would happen?!" I think it is a good trait for a counselor to be direct and honest, but to present that information in a tactful way. Let's use an example. Let's say you are counseling a 40-year-old married man with three kids. He tells you that he wants to stay married, he loves his wife dearly, and adores their life together but he feels like something is missing. A young woman at his work has been flirting with him and dropping hints that she would like to engage in an affair. He reports being torn because he feels something with this younger woman that he has not felt in a long time. As his counselor, it might feel good to say something like, "Hey you big dummy. Your wife is going to leave you if you sleep with that woman at work you have been thinking about. Duh!" And this is the sort of thing you might say to a friend, but remember that a counselor doesn't criticize. A counselor would say something like this: "I know you say you want to stay married, but if you continue to follow through with this affair then what is the likely outcome?" So, what is the difference between challenging and criticizing? Criticizing makes a person feel bad for what they did, and can oftentimes cause them to feel defensive. When you criticize someone, you point out their faults. When you challenge someone you only include facts, and there is no personal slant to it whatsoever. The following is a great sentence to remember and one that works great to challenge (I also used it above): "I know you say you want to do X, but if you continue to do Y, the likely outcome is Z."

Counselors Don't Fix Problems, But They Do Train Fixers
Why do people go to counseling? That's a great question, and there are several different answers. There are clients who come to counseling because someone made them; sometimes a judge, a spouse, a parent, or even an employer. However, a great majority of people seek out counseling because they need and want help. What do all these people have in common? There is a problem in their life and they cannot fix it themselves. Most people do not experience an issue for one day and then think, "Holy crap! I should see a counselor!" Most of the clients you see have likely been wrestling with their issues for years, exhausting all their own resources, and then finally seeking help outside of themselves or their support group. They want someone to swoop in, fix the problem, and exit just as fast as they came. Unfortunately, this is a common misconception about the counseling process. I'm about to say something that will shock you - the purpose of counseling is not to fix problems. Gasp! You might be thinking, "What are you talking about? Of course the purpose of counseling is to fix problems! Why else would people come to counseling if they don't need problems fixed?" People do need their problems fixed, but a counselor who "fixes" problems can oftentimes become do more damage than good, becoming more of an enabler than a helper. Allow me to explain myself. Remember the old adage about giving a man a fish versus teaching him how to fish? It goes like this: "Give a man a fish and he'll eat for a day; teach a man to fish and he'll eat for a lifetime." The man is hungry and he needs to eat. Giving him a fish seems like the civil and humane thing to do, but it's short-sighted. Fixing problems for clients is essentially giving them a fish. The job of a counselor is to teach clients how to fix their own problems. Why? Because there will always be more problems. If you fix one, more will pop up at some point. Your job as a counselor is to teach a person to fish. That means giving them the skills and support they need to make it on their own. This tenet of counseling goes back to not giving advice, because advice is how you fix a problem. Cultivate a problem-solving mindset with your clients, treat their illness, and confidently end your services knowing that they can catch their own fish.

PART II

It All Makes Sense...In Theory

Psychological theories are kind of like professional sports teams or popular television shows and movies. Star Wars and Star Trek die-hards are both really into the Science Fiction genre, but if you start a conversation about who was better between Captain Kirk and Obi-Wan Kenobi, they might just kill each other. The same thing with Chicago Bears fans and Green Bay Packers fans. They both love sports, but they will NEVER agree about the who the greatest team of all time is. Both are right and both are wrong; it all depends on your viewpoint. There are a lot of counseling theories - way more than I care to list. And each theory has a base of fans (practitioners) who follow the theory closely and will argue to no end the merits of their theory over any other. Is one more right than the other? Maybe. That's why they're called theories; no one really knows. The most important theory is the one that speaks to you, the one that you truly believe in. Why? Because a therapist who believes in his or her interventions is the one who often gets the best results. Your theory is important; believing in your theory is most important. When studying the different theories, you will likely find one that you are drawn to, one that seems to make more sense than the others. This is because of your unique life experiences and personality. One is not better than the other; they're just different.

CHAPTER 5

YOUR THEORETICAL ORIENTATION

Psychology is not an exact science; in fact, it's nowhere close. There are not many hard and fast "facts" that we can draw upon in the field of psychology. We know, for the most part, how the body works. A person can study medicine and learn what they need to know about the body - there aren't 500 theories about how and why the body works. We also know a lot about how the brain works, and when I use the word "brain" I am talking about the actual physical structure that is our brain. Neurologists have spent a great deal of their life learning about how the brain works and devoting their professional careers to learning more and helping people. The mind (which is the workings of the brain, or the psychology) on the other hand? We don't know anything. We think we might know some things, but those things we think we might know are mostly based on observations of large groups of people over long periods of time. We have noticed patterns and lumped those patterns into generalizations. This is a good thing because we now know more about the mind than we ever have, but do we have facts about how the mind works? Not really. What we do have is a bunch of theories (really, there are a ton of them) about how the mind works and why we do what we do. In the next few chapters I am going to cover some of the major theories, a little bit of their history, and some basics on their particular interventions. Note: I am not putting every detail about every theory or theorist here. That would be boring and you would fall asleep. What I have included is what I believe to be the key points and helpful interventions. Again, everyone has their own style.

When I was in graduate school and my professors would talk about picking a theory to practice I thought it was the coolest thing. I would learn about the theories, weigh their merit, and decide which one I liked. While this was awesome, it was also a little stressful. Here's a hint: don't freak out over picking a theory. You can pick and choose parts and pieces of different theories that best fit how you think you can help people. What worked for me was finding the theory I liked best and using that as my base for understanding how pathology is formed and where the deepest issues lie. I then pulled from several different theories to create a "toolbox" of interventions that can get to those root issues and truly help people. Here is a bit more advice though - know your theories, what theories you use, and why you use them. When a potential employer interviews you for a counseling position, chances are there will be a clinical supervisor (with a professional counseling license) who is a part of that process. That person will likely ask you about your theoretical orientation, and saying something like "I'm eclectic. I like many theories" sounds like you don't really know what you are talking about. You don't need to answer that question with a twenty-minute lecture on your theory including its founder and their biography, but you need to find some balance between those two possible answers. My answer would be "I practice with a Choice Theory/Reality Therapy base, and incorporate elements and interventions from Solution Focused, Cognitive Behavioral, and Existential Therapy to supplement treatment." Be prepared to answer a follow-up question about why you practice the theories you do, but your answers don't have to be especially long and you don't have to overstuff your response with fancy words. Your theoretical orientation is important, and something a clinical supervisor would likely want to know about.

CHAPTER 6

PSYCHOANALYTIC THEORY

Oh Sigmund Freud. It is arguable that no one has contributed more to the field of psychology than the guy I like to call Ole Siggy. However, If you interview 1,000 practicing counselors and/or psychologists, you will likely find 450 who praise Siggy for his contributions, 450 who believe he was a fraudulent sex-crazed egomaniac, and 100 who think he was just okay. Siggy is a very polarizing figure in psychology, in part because he was so highly praised for so long. Then more details about his life began to seep out and people began to question his theories and his methods. I didn't know Siggy personally (he died in 1939), so all my information comes from textbooks and other accounts. By all accounts he *was* an egomaniac who was also a workaholic (a lot of history's most successful geniuses were). And yes, looking through the lens of our current culture many of his ideas are now considered misogynistic and overly-focused on sex. It's hard to blame Siggy for this though, especially considering the time and culture in which he practiced. There was A LOT of sexual repression in that time and it is reasonable that a clinician would generalize a commonly seen symptom in many patients to *all* patients. So let's leave it at this - Freud was a great thinker who contributed tremendously to the field of psychology. Most of his stuff is fantastic, groundbreaking, and revolutionary. Some of it is just okay, and some of it is really weird. Let's talk about all of that.

Freud's unique brand of therapy has been called psychoanalysis, and the theory behind it is psychoanalytic theory. Freud theorized that personality is formed by the interactions between the three components of the human mind: the **id, ego, and superego**. The id wants what it wants, and it wants it right now. The id is primal, impulsive, and not governed by care for others or laws. The id has no concept of right or wrong; it only wants to be satisfied in the moment. The superego is on the opposite side of the spectrum from the id. The superego is overly concerned with societal norms and morals, even to the point of being irrational. The superego is what a lot of people would refer to as a conscience. And then there is the ego, or the "I". The ego is the balance between the id (biology) and the superego (society), concerning itself with pragmatic and rational thinking. The superego completely rejects the id, but the ego finds a way to satisfy the id through rational and acceptable ways. The ego is the negotiator. Freud believed that the id, ego, and superego are at constant odds with each other, with healthy people having a strong ego. Being overpowered by the id or the superego leads to neurosis (anxiety, depression, etc.).

The overarching theme of psychoanalysis is something Freud referred to as **the unconscious**. The unconscious is defined as the portion of your thinking and/or personality that you are not aware of. Problems with present functioning are almost always rooted in the unconscious mind. Past traumatic experiences and conflicts exist in the unconscious, and it is only the act of bringing those issues to the conscious mind that brings about resolution. So how do these conflicts get to the unconscious in the first place? Part of the ego's job is to protect itself from threats, psychological or otherwise. To do this, the ego employs what Freud dubbed **defense mechanisms**.

His defense mechanisms (stop me if you've heard these before) are repression, denial, projection, displacement, regression, sublimation, rationalization, and reaction formation (note - these are not all the defense mechanisms, just some of most prominent ones).

Repression - This is the act of simply hiding, or pushing down, negative thoughts, feelings, memories, and/or experiences to protect the conscious mind from the damage they may cause. An example would be an adult who was abused as a child and cannot recall a single detail of those events even though the person can recall other facts from their life at that time. This person has repressed those thoughts, feelings, and experiences to protect their conscious mind from the damage they could cause.

Denial - Denial and repression may seem the same on the surface, but there is one major difference. A person utilizing repression is completely unaware of what has happened, while a person in denial is aware of the situation but refusing to face the reality that the situation brings with it. An example would be a person who is going through a divorce and only shares happy feelings with family and close friends. It could be said that the person is in denial of the reality of their situation, refusing to address their grief.

Projection - Projection is attributing one's own thoughts, feelings, and motivations onto another person in order to protect oneself from the negative repercussions of said thoughts, feelings, and motivations. Let's say that Sally has strong negative feelings toward Alice, or in other words, Sally hates Alice. Alice's superego says "whoa, hate is wrong. You are supposed to like everyone." In response, Sally's ego creates a projection of those feelings to protect her psyche. Sally may genuinely believe that Alice hates her (whether she does or not) in order to normalize and rationalize her own feelings, thereby satisfying her superego.

Displacement - Displacement is when a person who is experiencing negative feelings towards someone or something expresses those feelings to someone or something else. Clear as mud? Here is an example. Billy-Bob is mad at his boss because his boss chewed him out today in front of the whole office. Billy-Bob cannot express this anger toward the person who made him angry (the boss) because he could be fired, so Billy-Bob comes home and is still mad as a hornet. Billy-Bob's three-year-old little boy (Bobby) spills his drink and Billy-Bob completely overreacts by screaming, yelling, and waving his hands wildly. Billy-Bob has just experienced displaced anger.

Regression - Regression is when a person's behaviors begin to mimic those of a much younger person. This is most commonly seen in children. A pre-teen may begin to wet the bed or suck their thumb in response to a traumatic event.

Sublimation - Sublimation is one of the only defense mechanisms to be considered somewhat healthy. Sublimation is similar to displacement, but an individual takes their feelings and channels them into something healthy or constructive. There are a lot of people who use anger and personal struggles to fuel their motivation for the arts and/or exercise. Let's say that Janice is unhappy in her marriage, and she feels a great deal of anger toward her husband. She does not feel that she can express this anger toward him because she is scared he will leave her. So what does she do? She channels that anger into jogging and lifting weights. That anger energizes her and allows her to accomplish something constructive she would not otherwise have been able to do. This defense mechanism is not entirely healthy (she still is not dealing with the real issue) but it is one of the few that can yield positive results.

Rationalization - This involves distorting the facts to make an event or a feeling seem less threatening. Let's say that Jessica's friend JoAnn is mean to her, to the point of almost being verbally abusive. When asked about this Jessica might say, "Well, JoAnn is under a lot of pressure. Her job is very demanding and that makes her a high-strung person who needs to vent sometimes." Jessica's ego has changed the facts (JoAnn is really mean and borderline abusive) to make the whole situation seem less threatening.

By employing these defense mechanisms (and many others) the ego can protect itself from threats, which is only natural. Defense mechanisms are not intentional and a person likely has no clue they are using them. The role of the therapist is to point out the use of these defense mechanisms, thereby bringing the unconscious to the conscious mind and starting the journey toward resolution. The unconscious, while mostly unknown by the conscious mind, does manage to slip out from time to time. These are what we would call **Freudian Slips**. A Freudian Slip (named that later, Freud called it a parapraxis) is when a person misspeaks, and that mistake reveals something about the unconscious. For example, a man may mean to say, "We are looking for the best and brightest" but actually say "We are looking for the breast and brightest". This is a hilarious slip of the tongue that most people would just laugh off (me included), but Freud would suggest that such a slip is no accident at all. In fact, he believed that this was the unconscious mind making its way to the surface.

The unconscious also makes itself known through dreams and therapeutic activities known as **projective tasks**. A projective task is an activity that gives the unconscious a chance to come out. One of these projective tasks is called **free association**. In free association, the therapist recites a list of words and the client responds with whatever comes to their mind first, not filtering any of the answers. The idea is that the unconscious can be brought to the surface through an exercise such as free association. Another projective task (where the client *projects* their own interpretation onto something) is ink blots, also called **Rorschach Ink Blots**. These ink blots are ambiguous which means that they don't have an actual form or represent a specific picture. The client will look at the inkblot and state what they think it is, or, project their own thoughts/feelings onto the picture. This activity again gives the therapist (and the client) some insight into the workings of the client's unconscious mind.

Freud considered dreams to be the primary source of understanding a person's unconscious mind. He believed that the ego had difficulties suppressing feelings and memories while a person slept, so the unconscious can act without interference in dreams. The unconscious does not allow our desires to be spelled out in exact pictures of what we want, but rather uses metaphors that require interpretation. Thus, **dream analysis** is an intervention frequently used in psychotherapy.

Another of Freud's major contributions to psychology was the concept of **transference and countertransference.** Transference is the phenomenon where a person transfers feelings about another person or situation onto a different person or situation. Transference is something that happens many times in the therapeutic relationship. A male client who is seeing a female therapist for marital problems may begin to interpret the therapist as "sounding like my wife" throughout the course of treatment. Likewise, a female client who has issues with her father may begin to seek approval from an older male therapist. Countertransference occurs when the therapist transfers feelings onto a client. Countertransference often occurs as a reaction to transference, but transference is not necessary for countertransference. Countertransference can be helpful or harmful to the therapeutic relationship, and the psychoanalyst believes that these feelings need to be explored.

There is enough information on psychoanalytic theory to fill numerous textbooks, and what I have covered only scratches the surface. Psychoanalytic theory is one of the first, most researched, and most vetted theories out there.

CHAPTER 7

ADLERIAN THERAPY

Alfred Adler is called the father of individual psychology, and you don't get a nickname like that for average contributions to the field. Adler was a medical doctor and a therapist who lived from 1870 to 1935. He studied with Sigmund Freud and the two of them, along with a couple of other folks, began the psychoanalytic movement. Adler saw the world and psychology differently than Freud did, and the two parted ways after a couple of years working together. Freud tended to see people as an island unto themselves, and his psychoanalytic theory matched his perception. Adler took more of a holistic approach, focusing on how the person functions in their family, community, and beyond. One way to put it is that Freud fit people into his psychoanalytic theory, while Adler fit his theory around the individual person and their needs. This way of seeing people is called a phenomenological approach. By the way, phenomenological is probably my favorite word in the English language. Alfred Adler saw the therapist and client as being equals, eschewing the Freudian couch for two chairs.

In Adlerian therapy, family of origin plays a huge role. Adler was one of the first to believe strongly in personality, and he developed his own theory of how personality is formed. He believed that social constructs were the primary motivation for human behavior, and a person begins to form their approach to life within their first six years. Have you ever heard of the term

inferiority complex? That came from Adler. He believed that feelings of inferiority were not only normal, but the source of all motivation. While feeling inferior can certainly be seen as a precursor to negative feelings, Adler flipped this thinking around. He believed that feeling inferior was also a driving force for superiority, and motivation for improvement comes from these feelings.

Adler believed that personality, or the way a person "goes about living", is both created by and is creating the individual at the same time. Thus, a person is in control of their own destiny. This personality, the way a person goes about life, was called a person's **lifestyle**. Adler believed that a person's lifestyle is their core beliefs, assumptions, and what drives their everyday decisions. Your lifestyle begins to form when you are very young, and every social interaction has some influence on your lifestyle. As you gain more experience you begin to generalize similar experiences into basic rules, or assumptions, about life. If a child really wants some candy, what will they do? They will probably ask, or grab it themselves. If they are told no by their parents they might cry, yell, or throw a tantrum. If the tantrum results in the child getting what they want, they have learned something. "If I make enough noise and make everyone around me uncomfortable, I get what I want." If that behavior continues to be reinforced it is safe to assume that the child will develop this assumption and generalize it to other aspects of their life. They might have tantrums every time they don't get their way, and many of us have experienced adults who have the same assumption. This is an example of how early social experiences can influence a person's perception and lifestyle.

Family of origin has the greatest impact on a person's lifestyle. A family has many rules, both spoken and unspoken. These rules oftentimes become the way a child sees and determines how a life should be lived. Think about it. Who handled the money in your home? Who made the decisions regarding discipline? Who had the final say during difficult times? Who cooked dinner? Who worked? Who picked up the kids? Who did yard work? Were there times when you could and could not speak with your mom? Your dad? All these things (and many more) play into how a child develops a view of life. Adler saw **birth order** as being a major factor as well. He saw patterns of personality with people and was able to generalize a lot of those traits to their birth order. Many of these traits develop out of a response to how parents treat different children, and some traits develop in relation to other siblings. Let me explain.

He noticed that *oldest child* tended to be a perfectionist, hard-working, and stubborn. An oldest child bears the responsibility of being the first-born and often having to help care for younger siblings. Parents tend to have high expectations for a first-born and are a bit stricter. Oldest children will often-times become strict rule followers themselves.

The *second child* in a set of two is many times overly-competitive. They have feel that they are at constant odds with the oldest child and competing for love and attention. A second child may also develop a rebellious attitude, and often times is opposite in personality from the first born.

The *middle child* tends to be the diplomat, or the peace-maker. Middle children many times have difficulty defining their place within the family, and later, society. They do not receive the attention and responsibility of the oldest, but also do not receive the doting of the youngest. Learning to negotiate and please others is central to a middle child's typical tendencies. They are easy going and pleasant to get along with. There are many middle children who are what you would call "people pleasers", as they seek to avoid conflict at all costs.

The *youngest child* is many times the most pampered and attended to. They are the babies of the family and receive the most attention. They tend to be risk takers and have outgoing personalities. They are often described as charming, manipulative, spoiled, impatient, and persistent.

The *only child* is a special breed. Many only children grow up preferring adult interactions and using adult language (having not interacted with many children at home). Only children tend to be independent and have no problems caring for themselves. They also can be assertive and pragmatic.

These birth order traits and characteristics are not hard and fast rules, but generalizations typically seen. Not EVERY child fits into one of these categories, but think about your siblings or other sibling groups you know. Do you know some who fit? I have had countless parents come and talk to me informally, saying, "I'm worried about my 10-year-old. He is stubborn, a perfectionist, a rule follower, and he makes himself anxious worrying about responsibilities he doesn't even have." My next question is, "Is he your oldest child?" Almost always they would say, "Well, yeah". Then we would discuss birth order and how some of those traits are typical of a first-born. Reading through Adler's theory on birth order and how family of origin affects a person's lifestyle, you begin to see patterns in your own life and the lives of others. He was on to something.

Adler called our perceptions regarding ourselves, others, and society **private logic**. Private logic is basically the core values, thoughts, or assumptions we developed in our lifestyle. As individuals, Adler saw people as having problems when their private logic did not line up with societal norms or the logic of others. Adler saw great value in asking about early childhood experiences. Not to glean what happened or gain an understanding of how the family worked, but to gauge the client's perspective. An effective question would be, "What is your earliest childhood memory?" The actual memory and what was going on is not all that important, but the client's perception is key to understanding their lifestyle. When the client describes the memory, pay close attention to the details and ask follow-up questions if needed. Who was there? What was happening? What were the other people doing? Who was closest to the client? Who was furthest away? Our memories (especially early childhood ones) are not typically accurate and tend to become shaded by our perception, so all of these details are important. While a psychoanalyst may ask questions about early childhood to uncover a traumatic event, an Adlerian therapist asks these questions to better understand the individual, their perception of themselves, and their perception of their place in society.

CHAPTER 8

PERSON CENTERED THERAPY

Carl Rogers (1902-1987) developed what is known as Person Centered Therapy. This type of therapy draws heavily on humanistic psychology and focuses on the person. Rogers believed in people; he believed they were essentially good and possess the ability to resolve their own issues. This believe in the client as already possessing the capacity for self-improvement was in stark contrast with many early theorists. Rogers also turned the therapy world upside down by challenging the overarching sentiment regarding the role of the therapist in the therapeutic relationship. Rogers believed that the therapist's attitude and their relationship with the client was far more important than the therapist's knowledge of theory and techniques. He also stated that the goal of therapy is not to solve problems, but to help each client in their growth process so they could solve their own problems. The focus of therapy is the individual, not the presenting problem.

Rogers put the onus on the therapist to engage each and every client in a real relationship, and not keep clients at a cold and calculated distance. It is in the relationship that the client can find within themselves the capacity for change that was there all along. The therapeutic relationship must consist of these core conditions - congruence, unconditional positive regard, and empathy.

Congruence means being real. As therapists, and anyone in a helping relationship, we tend to distance ourselves from the reality of what our clients are facing. We see so many people and bear so many burdens that a natural coping skill is to distance ourselves, to see the client as machinery that needs fixing. We run the risk of losing our humanity in our interactions with our clients and everything we do sounds like we are a therapy-bot. Congruence, also called genuineness, means you have to be an actual human being. Don't put up a professional front that makes you seem all-knowing (you are not), completely in control of all your emotions (you are not), and the keeper of how to live a happy life (you are not). Be real, but remember that like all important traits, this one exists on a continuum; it is not all or nothing. You can be genuine, but don't overshare or blab about how terrible you are. There is a balance that must be struck, but you must be authentic and be your real self… no therapy-bots.

Unconditional positive regard is basically a fancy way of saying that you accept the client as who they are, no matter what. This attitude is one that does not convey judgement or criticism, but an open and honest caring for another. One misconception with this is that you have to be approving of every behavior, no matter how destructive. Unconditional positive regard does not mean that you approve of every behavior or that you never challenge your client. It means that your acceptance of who they are has no conditions, no strings attached to it. While you may need to challenge their thoughts or actions, you do so in a caring way.

Empathy is an understanding of who the client and what they are experiencing. Many times, we get empathy and sympathy confused, but they are quite different. Sympathy is feeling bad or sorry for someone, but empathy is feeling what they feel. It is putting yourself in their shoes and understanding their story from their perspective. Empathy is something some people are naturally better at than others, but it is still a skill that can be improved. Empathy takes practice. If empathy can truly be cultivated in the therapeutic relationship, the chances of client success are improved dramatically.

The person-centered approach to therapy does not include a list of techniques and strategies, but rather focuses on the interactions and the quality of the relationship between the therapist and the client. If the therapist can bring the core conditions for change into the session, the client has a great chance of having success. Remember, person centered therapy asserts that the client has within themselves the capacity for positive change; they just need someone to help guide them through that process.

CHAPTER 9

CHOICE THEORY/REALITY THERAPY

Full disclosure: this is my theory. Reality Therapy (and its guiding principles of Choice Theory) speaks to me. So, if you read this and think, "Man, this guy is really biased in favor of this theory", it's true. William Glasser (1925-2013) is the man behind Choice Theory and Reality Therapy. Choice Theory, originally called Control Theory, is the foundation for the practice of Reality Therapy. Choice Theory states that everything you do is a choice - everything. From the moment you wake up until the second you fall asleep you make hundreds if not thousands of decisions. So many of our choices happen in a nanosecond or are so habitual that we do not even realize we have a choice, but if we stopped to think we would realize we are truly in control of our own lives - and have no control over the lives of others. A mantra of Choice Theory is "I am responsible for my own behaviors. I can control myself, but I cannot control anyone else." Stress, anxiety, and other disorders are often rooted in a futile attempt to control the uncontrollable (other people), or a feeling that we are not in control of our own lives. Choice theory is about giving control to the one person who truly has it - the individual.

Glasser believed that all people had the same five basic psychological needs, and fulfilling or protecting those needs was the basis for behavior. The areas of psychological need are **love/belonging** - fitting in, being with a family, friends, or a community; **freedom/independence** - to have your own personal space, control over your life, and the ability to make your own choices; **power/accomplishment** - having a sense of achievement, accomplishing a goal, having self-worth; **fun** - recreation and enjoyment; **survival** - shelter, food, to continue living. These needs are not specific, but very general. This means that **perception** plays a huge role in Choice Theory/Reality Therapy. I think roller coasters are awesome, and they would fulfill my need for fun. However, I have friends who find roller coasters terrifying, and riding one threatens their need for survival. Glasser also believed that these needs do not exist on a hierarchy as you would see with Maslow's work, but are more analogous to the legs on a chair. The needs work in harmony and each one is as important as the other. Glasser used the analogy of a thermostat to highlight how the needs work in conjunction with our functioning. In his analogy, the brain is the thermostat and the needs have temperatures. When we perceive that one of our needs is in need of fulfillment or is being threatened, our brain kicks on and tells our body and/or mind to do something. And the reaction that ensues is a **total behavior** reaction.

Total behavior includes actions, thoughts, feelings, and physiology. Actions, thoughts, and feelings are self-explanatory, but you might not know what physiology is. Physiology is your body's response to stimuli. We have physiological responses to a lot of different situations that we might not realize. When we become angry or frightened our body pumps out adrenaline to prepare for fight or flight. The physiological response is that you feel more energy and you might be shaky, short of breath, or fidgety. When you are hungry your stomach might growl - that is another physiological response. There are only two parts of total behavior that we have control over - our actions and thoughts. All four components of total behavior are connected and they cannot be separated; a change in one leads to a response from all of them. It is helpful to think of the four components of total behavior as being like the four wheels of a car. All the wheels are connected to each other by the frame of the car and axles. When you decide to move the car in one way or another you turn the steering wheel. The steering wheel only controls the front two wheels, but wherever they go the rear wheels have no choice but to follow. The front wheels are your thoughts and actions, while the back wheels are your feelings and physiology. You have control over the rear wheels (feelings and physiology), but only indirectly and by controlling the front wheels.

If we take this concept of total behavior we see that reality therapy is both action oriented and insight oriented, depending on which area the client is more willing to make a change. A change in behavior will lead to a change in thinking, feeling, and physiology. Likewise, a change in thinking will lead to a change in behavior, feeling, and physiology. It is inconsequential which is change first, as a change in any area will lead to a change in all areas.

The **WDEP model** was developed as part of the Reality Therapy process. W = Wants, D = Doing/Direction, E = self-Evaluation, P = Planning. "What do you want?" is a question you will hear posed a lot (and in several different ways) during the course of treatment. It is common for a therapist to start a session with "what do want to get out of our visit today?" But asking what a person wants is usually not enough. There needs to be some exploration and soul searching to find out what it is a person wants. Wants tend to exist at different levels of motivation, and a person is only likely to get that which they want the most. "What do you want?" tends to be a loaded question. After wants are established, the therapist will ask "what are you doing?" or "which direction are you moving in?" Establishing what the client behaviors will likely create a discrepancy between the stated wants and current actions. The next step is self-evaluation, and this step is the most crucial in the process. "Is what you are currently doing moving you closer to your wants or further from them?" Another way to ask this is, "If you continue acting exactly as you have been and change nothing, what is the likely outcome?" This self-evaluation is hard and takes some real soul-searching on the part of the client. The only way a person can change is if they first decide that a change is more advantageous. The therapist will challenge whether or not the client truly wants what they say they want, and guide them on how to make changes to start moving in the right direction; that's where the planning phase comes in. With the help of the therapist, the client makes a plan to start moving in the direction of their wants. This movement in a satisfactory direction brings about need fulfillment and moves the total behavior system in a positive way. The WDEP model takes time, at least several sessions to complete. It does not need to be hurried or rushed through, as a superficial self-evaluation or determination of wants will not yield the most positive results.

Reality therapists take a "look, but don't stare" approach to the past. They are focused on the present, the here and now. A reality therapist wants to know about your past, but only to inform them on how to assist you in the present. Much of therapy is focused on teaching the client the basics of choice theory and reality therapy, exploring client perceptions, need fulfillment, and total behavior patterns. A reality therapist will then work the client on creating an intervention that is aimed at changing one area of total behavior in order to bring about change in the entire system. Change begets change.

CHAPTER 10

SOLUTION FOCUSED THERAPY

Solution Focused Therapy is one of the most unique approaches to counseling we have, and it is relatively new. It was developed in the late 1970s by Steve DeShazer (1940-2005) and Insoo Kim Berg (1934-2007). What happens when a person enters therapy? Typically, the client will sit across from a therapist and begin sharing about why they came, also known as the presenting problem. In Solution Focused Therapy the client would sit across from the therapist and the therapist might ask, "What's going right with your life?" So much of therapy is problem focused, which many would argue leads to further client suffering. Therapists ask clients to describe their problems with as much detail as possible. The therapist then picks, sorts, and pulls apart individual facets of each problem for examination. Many believed it was time for a new approach.

Solution Focused Therapy, as the name implies, is focused on finding solutions. What would happen if a person moved from using the language of problems to the language of solutions? Furthermore, what could be accomplished if a therapist worked toward building the innate strengths that a client has? Solution Focused Therapy is largely based on skillful questioning, building on client strengths, and helping an individual move toward specific solutions. The focus is on the here and now, not on past experiences. The focus is realistic goals and building positive momentum.

The Miracle Question

The miracle question is one of the most useful therapeutic tools there is, and variations of this intervention can be found all over. The therapist asks the client to indulge them while they ask a fantastical question that requires them to use their imagination: "Let's say that while you were sleeping tonight a miracle occurred, and when you woke up your problem (the presenting problem) was gone. But because you were sleeping you are unaware that a miracle occurred. As you slowly begin to wake up, what is the first sign that would show you a miracle occurred?" Their answer will tell you a lot about their goals, their perception of both their problem and themselves, and how much insight they have into their issue. The question can then be expanded to include others as well. "How would your spouse (and/or children) know that this miracle happened?" is a great question to help start the development of goals. The miracle question can be followed up by a nearly infinite amount of questions, but this typically leads the therapist perfectly into goal setting. "How realistic is it that this 'miracle' could occur?" "If you were to make one small step this week toward making this miracle scenario a reality, what would that be?" Do you see what I mean!? This one miracle question is a great segway to goal setting, treatment planning, and the entire counseling process.

Scaling Questions

Scaling questions are great because they take what is abstract and difficult to define, and provides some level of concreteness. So much of mental health is subjective that it can be difficult, if not impossible, to measure. If a client sits across from you and says, "I feel anxious", you have no way to quantify that. Treatment planning, measuring outcomes, and determining the overall helpfulness of therapy can be maddening. Enter scaling questions! Scaling questions involve putting something on a scale (usually small numbers like 1-10 or 1-5) and measuring progress based on that scale. Asking a client to assign a number on a scale to their issue or level of discomfort is still largely subjective, but you might be surprised at the insight a scale can provide. A scaling question might go something like this, in which the therapist would say, "You have told me today about some anxiety you have been feeling that is making it difficult for you to function in your family and your work. If you had to put your average daily comfort level with your anxiety on a scale of 1-10, with 1 being no comfort at all and 10 being the most comfortable and relaxed, where would you be?" Their answer, again, will give you (and them) a ton of insight into how they feel about their problem and their perception of the scope of their issue. Scaling questions are another great way to make goals, create treatment plans, and measure continued progress. Not only that, but scaling questions provide an opportunity to build on strengths. Let's say that the client stated, "I would rate my comfort level related to my anxiety at a 4." As a therapist you could say, "Wow. A 4?! That's really great. Based on everything you are going through right now I thought that number might be lower. What things have you done to keep yourself from being a 3?" By making that statement you are engaging in Solution Focused Therapy by building on positives, being complementary, and asking the client what has been working for them. Moving forward, goal setting can look like this, as the therapist might say, "What would life look like for you if you were at a 5? Between today and next week I want you to think about what one small change you could make to help be a 4.5." And boom! It's a beautiful thing. Assigning a number to a symptom is helpful for both the client and the therapist throughout treatment. Throughout each session (in fact sometimes during a session) you will want to check in and see where their number is. Did it go up? Did it go down? Why? Can we identify and replicate the successes? What can we change to limit the negatives? Scaling questions are loaded with opportunity.

Exception Questions
There is almost no problem that is present at full intensity 24 hours a day, 7 days a week. Even the most persistent depression and/or anxiety is not with a person all the time. That's where exception questions come in. A therapist may ask, "When is your problem not a problem? Can you remember the last time you did not have _____ going on?" They might say, "No", and require a little more probing. At the very least you can get them to scale and then

describe times when the problem is least intense. "When is the problem not a problem?" The answer to this question gives the client a hope that they might not have realized was there. So much time is spent dwelling on this issue that it genuinely FEELS like it is everywhere all the time. Exception questions highlight client strengths and give the client/therapist a chance to identify successful treatment regimens. Let's continue our example of the client who comes in with severe anxiety. They might answer an exception question by saying, "Well, the other day at work I gave a presentation and my boss told me I did a really great job. I felt so good for the next few hours and didn't really have any anxiety." That's a great springboard for a conversation about self-esteem, praise from others, and how the person views himself or herself. This could lead into a deeper discussion, such as, "Think back to other times you received praise and felt like you did a good job. Was your anxiety less in those times as well?" or "How does criticism affect your anxiety level?" When you are looking for exceptions, find out where the client was, what was happening, who was with them, and what their mood was before/during/after. All of these answers are potential clues to the problem solution that is already within the client - they just don't know it's there.

Coping Questions

Almost no one makes an appointment for therapy the very first time they experience something such as anxiety, depression, or marital issues. The decision to seek out help usually happens after a person feels that they have exhausted all of their personal resources to handle the issue. In that time of running through their own resiliency, people tend to develop coping skills. Some coping skills, and some...not so much. So, people cope with depression by exercising (typically good) and some cope with alcohol (probably not the best idea). The point is that people have built in mechanisms for handling their issues and (if their coping skills are healthy) the therapist will want to build on what is already there rather than starting from scratch. The coping skills a person employs are likely things that they enjoy or are good at, and they may just need help developing those skills or applying them to specific issues.

CHAPTER 11

COGNITIVE BEHAVIORAL THERAPY

Cognitive behavioral therapy (CBT) was developed in the 1960s by Aaron Beck, who was a psychiatrist. Since that time CBT has grown to become one of the most recognized and widely used therapeutic techniques we have. CBT posits that we have literally thousands of thoughts running through our minds all day every day. These thoughts, typically based on personal experience and exposed to our own bias, tend to occur in patterns and we generalize those patterns into attitudes or beliefs about ourselves. Life is less about what happens to us and more about how we perceive and interpret those events. These thought patterns are natural and something that everyone engages in, but issues arrive when those thoughts, attitudes, or beliefs are based on faulty assumptions or irrational thoughts. Those irrational thoughts lead to problematic behavior, broken relationships, an unrealistic self-image, and a litany of other mental health concerns.

Those issues tend to persist unless the pattern of irrational thinking can be broken, challenged, or in any way interrupted. Those negative and unrealistic patterns of thinking are called **cognitive distortions**. There are many types of different cognitive distortions, and here are a few:

1) All or Nothing Thinking: The world is seen through the lens of absolutes. Words like "always" "never" "everyone" and "no one" are a

part of your vocabulary. There is no middle ground and one negative event is seen as a predestined pattern.

2) Filtering: When a situation occurs and the good or potential is left out of your thought processes – you filter out the good and only focus on the bad or potential bad.

3) Overgeneralization: One bad situation or one skill in which you are lacking is then generalized to your whole personality and who you are as an individual.

4) Shoulds and Musts: Faulty thinking (usually from childhood) on what ourselves or another person "should" or "must" do.

5) Mind Reading: The assumption that (A) others are thinking/talking about you and (B) the topic is negative.

6) Jumping to Conclusions: Allowing emotions to control your perception of events instead of rational thoughts. i.e., "she did not bring me lunch today – she must hate me!"

7) Labeling: Demeaning yourself by using negative self-labels after an event. You may call yourself "fat" or "stupid" or "loser". These labels become ingrained and create a false self-image.

Cognitive behavioral therapy won't change ingrained faulty thoughts overnight, but it works more quickly than you might think. A person has typically spent their entire life developing their pattern of thinking, and in many cases, they have deeply ingrained beliefs based on those thoughts. The good news is that it does not take nearly as long to undo those patterns as it did to create them. One break in the pattern or one rational and well-balanced thought can do wonders for a person's psyche. Positive thinking can build momentum just as quickly as negative thinking.

It can be easy to identify surface level cognitive distortions, such as "I don't look pretty" or "I will fail at my job", but helping a client uncover a core belief can be more difficult. This takes time, practice, and some insight on the part of the therapist and the client. Oftentimes a surface level cognitive distortion is an outgrowth of a faulty belief. "I will fail at my job" is a thought process that comes about because a person may believe "I am not good enough to do anything well". A core belief such as that will result in faulty thinking in many areas of a person's life. Being presented with actual evidence that a core belief may not be true can begin to chip away at those faulty beliefs.

CHAPTER 12

EXISTENTIAL THERAPY

Existential therapy, simply put, is meaning therapy. The focus of existential therapy is on the human experience as a whole rather than focusing on individual aspects. This form of therapy was born out of the work of philosophers Friedrich Nietzsche and Soren Kierkegaard. This philosophy has since been developed and worked into a therapeutic framework by the likes of Rollo May, Irvin Yalom, and Viktor Frankl. Existential therapists believe that there are certain conditions that are inherent to the human experience, and conflict with these conditions bring about distress. Four of these conditions are: freedom (and the responsibility it brings), death, isolation, and meaninglessness. A person has to face these conditions and accept them in a healthy way to find a sense of purpose.

Existential therapy is philosophical in nature, and applying this form of therapy has to be done with a client who is a) willing to engage in philosophy and b) has the capacity to think on this type of level. The approach is almost entirely intellectual and this provides some limitations to its application. However, the guiding principles and ideas can be some of the powerful and motivating in the entire field of psychology. Existential therapy is filled with positivity, overcoming, finding purpose, and becoming something better than you have been before.

Consider the story of Viktor Frankl, who created Logotherapy (meaning therapy) and was a major contributor to the field of existential therapy. He was an Austrian neurologist and psychiatrist who was also a holocaust survivor. His book, "Man's Search for Meaning" is his story of surviving in a concentration camp and his subsequent creation of Logotherapy. His story is equal parts heartbreaking, inspiring, and motivating. He had everything taken from him, and when only the barest of human experience was left, he found meaning. Through this meaning he was able to channel his suffering into inspiration and overcame one of the most horrible tragedies in human history.

Existential therapy does not have specific techniques or homework assignments for clients, but it involves a true introspection of the meaning of life, the human existence, and our individual place in the grand scheme. Many people, especially those who come to therapy, have struggled with existential angst - questions like "What's the meaning of life?" "Is there a point to all this?" "Why do I have to suffer?" can be discussed and hopefully resolved using existential therapy.

Remember that there are plenty of successful therapists who only practice psychoanalysis, plenty of successful therapists who only practice Adlerian therapy, plenty of successful therapists who only practice reality therapy, etc. There are therapists who are successful with every major theory. This is just me thinking out loud, but if all these different theories and approaches to the human psyche have been successful with at least a small multitude of people, was Carl Rogers right? Are the three core conditions all that is needed for the client to have success in therapy? That is a question no one can definitively answer, but it is a conclusion I draw toward more and more as I continue in this line of work. The attitude and approach of the therapist is way more important than the theory or the intervention. Remember that as you consider theories and how you want to practice.

PART III

IN THE SESSION

Okay, so this is the most intimidating part of counseling (for me at least) - the actual counseling. This part of the book will focus on the actual skills and knowledge needed for counseling individuals, as well as provide practical advice for navigating the counseling relationship.

CHAPTER 13

THE FIRST SESSION

The first session you have with a client will be very different than any subsequent session. The first session is usually when you review informed consent, get the signatures you need, go over expectations for counseling, and field any questions the client may have. Informed consent is very important and something that must be done in order to protect you and the client.

Informed Consent

Informed consent is where you lay it all out there for the client. This is the opportunity for them to know everything that's going to happen so they can back out if they want to and they are not surprised by the counseling process. The client will sign the informed consent stating that they understand what they are getting into and they can't claim ignorance of the process down the road. Your informed consent needs to be iron-clad, and that's for a couple of reasons. The first reason is that it is your responsibility to your clients to help them understand exactly what they are getting into when they come for counseling. They need to know the risks, the limitations, and how the process works. The second reason is for litigation. If you have a poorly written informed consent, i.e. you leave a bunch of stuff off of there, you make yourself vulnerable to a lawsuit if a client becomes upset. A good informed consent includes the following:

- Who you are and your qualifications: You cannot exaggerate, lie, or bend the truth in any way. Your client needs to know exactly who you are and why you are qualified to provide this service. If you are one day from getting your PhD, you cannot call yourself a PhD; wait until tomorrow. State your name, the degree you achieved, and any relevant experience.

- The risks vs. the benefits of therapy: Yes, there are risks to therapy. And your client needs to know what those risks are. Therapy is something that is deeply personal, and typically (if done right) has involves A LOT of introspective and soul searching. Therapy tends to invoke change; change brings risk. A person may spend time in therapy and decide to end their marriage (even though marriage may never come up in session), a person may decide to sever certain relationships, change jobs, or generally change their outlook on life. Your clients need to know that this may happen. When you begin to speak with a client about deep, personal pain there is often a worsening of symptoms before they begin to get better. This stinks, but it is part of the process. Again, putting this in your informed consent fulfills two obligations. You are protecting the client by letting them know ahead of time, and you are also protecting yourself against possible litigation.

- Confidentiality (and its limits): This is huge; the future of your practice, professional reputation, and your livelihood may very well depend on whether or not you cover confidentiality. As a mental health counselor, your client's information is protected by HIPAA (Health Insurance Portability and Accountability Act). As a counselor, you cannot go home and tell your wife, "Wow. Johnny Smith is having trouble with depression. Did you know his wife left him?" the same way your doctor couldn't say, "Hey honey, do you know Johnny Smith? Yeah, those genital warts are back again. That's the third time for him!" Information disclosed in counseling is considered medical information, and disclosing confidential information can have serious ramifications. That being said, there are limits to the confidentiality of the relationship and it is vital that your client know what those limits are. If a client discloses child or elder abuse, abandonment, or neglect then you report it to the proper authorities. If a client discloses information that, in your professional judgement, deems them an immediate threat to their own safety or the safety of others, then you have to report that. Let me break that one down for you a little: if they are suicidal or homicidal you must do something about it. Some states have varying laws on what should or should not be reported, and the details are something you need to know if you plan on practicing counseling. Another limit to confidentiality would be a court order - and this happens. Let's say you are providing anger management counseling for Jimmy John. Jimmy John's wife, Jan John, leaves him and wants full custody of the children, stating that Jimmy John is emotionally unstable. You may be called to testify or your records might be subpoenaed, as you are Jimmy John's counselor and an expert on his emotional health. This does not happen all the time, but it does happen. The key is that your clients need to know about these limits to confidentiality going in. You likely live in the town you will be practicing mental health. What happens if you run into your client Julie in the grocery store and she is there with her friends? This sounds silly, but it's smart to prepare your client for this potential situation - BECAUSE IT HAPPENS. You can't say, "Hey Julie! Nice to see you!" even though that would be common courtesy. If you say hi to Julie, then you have told her family that you know her. When they ask how she knows you (and they will ask) she will either have to lie or share that you are her counselor. It is not her friend's business whether or not she is in counseling, unless Julie decides to tell them. Prepare your client for a potential situation like that by saying, "If I run into you anywhere in town I will not speak to you. It is not because I want to be rude, but because I want to protect your confidentiality. I would love to chat with you, but you would have to be the one to initiate the conversation." Putting it that way puts the onus on the client - after all, you are not a heartless jerk who refuses to speak to people in public. You would be more than happy to talk with Julie, but to protect her confidentiality she needs to give the okay for a conversation to take place.

- Your theoretical orientation: Why is this important? For one thing, it conveys a sense of professionalism and expertise to your clients; the more they believe in you and what you are doing, the more likely it is that counseling will be successful for them. Why else? Because your clients have a right to know what you are doing and why you are doing it. You should have a conviction about your methods and their roots; you need to believe in your process.

- The process of counseling (how long it takes, what to do if you don't like it, etc.): Most people who come to counseling do not have a clue what to expect. They might have done a little internet research, but the rest of their knowledge is likely from TV or something they may have heard from their friends. Your clients need to know that counseling is not supposed to be a lifelong endeavor; it has a beginning, middle, and end. They need to know that the two of you are a team working for their benefit. They need to understand that if they do not like some aspect of counseling they need to share it. They need to know that they have not entered a long-term contract and they can end counseling whenever they want. The process needs to be explained because the average person just does not know.

- Expectations for client and counselor: This is a portion of informed consent that is often overlooked. You and the client need to go over the expectations you have for one another. As a counselor, you would expect your client to show up for appointments, call if they can't, and treat you with respect. Likewise, the client has the right to know that they can have the same expectations of you. Your client can expect you to be on time for appointments, promptly contact if a cancellation is needed, and they can also expect to be treated with respect.

This provides a wonderful opportunity to discuss any preconceived ideas one person may have about the other and negotiate expectations for the counseling relationship.

- Fee schedule: Your client needs to know up front what counseling will cost, when you will bill them, and what the fee policy is for missed appointments. It can be uncomfortable, but lay it all out there. Putting the information out in the first session is far less discomforting than charging a no-show fee and having the client say, "You never told me about that!"

- Insurance billing: If you bill insurance for your services, explain to your client what that means. Their information is protected by HIPAA, but the insurance company sees the information. Most insurance companies require a DSM diagnosis for services, and many people are not comfortable receiving a diagnosis.

- Making/cancelling appointments: If you made it this far you have a policy on this - share it with your client. Do you require 24 hour notice to cancel an appointment without a fee? Is a text message or email sufficient communication to cancel? Do future appointments have to be scheduled after every session or should they be expected the next week at the same time?

- Contact information/what do in an emergency: Your clients need to be able to contact you. Give them a phone number, email address, fax number, etc. Be very specific about your policy regarding contact hours. This becomes important when a client may want to call and chat with you at 10 PM about an emergency. It might be a true emergency and they might really need help, but you must establish boundaries. Your clients can leave you a voicemail, but if they are in a true emergency they need to call 911. A rational thinking person knows this, but you must spell it out to protect yourself.

- Other rights: Cover any other rights your client might have and any questions. They have a right to their records, they can bring anyone they want into a counseling session, etc.

Intake Paperwork:

Aside from reviewing the informed consent, the initial session (and in some cases this can be done prior to the initial session) should include the completion and review of the client information and history. This is where you get all the background information you need to move forward with counseling. If you are in private practice, this is where solid preparation will pay off. You need to have these forms developed and ready to go before your first client calls. If you work in an agency or for another private practitioner, they will likely have forms in place already. This form is where you will get the demographic information, relationship status, health/medical background, substance use information, familial history of medical, substance, or mental health issues, current job status, etc. This form is yours and can be formatted in any way, but you have to have one to make sure you get an accurate picture of the client. If you are not sure what to put in your intake packet a quick Google search will give you a pretty good idea. This intake packet is often referred to as a Biopsychosocial Assessment (BPSA) by many practitioners and insurance companies.

CHAPTER 14

DIAGNOSING

So, you made it through the informed consent and you are now ready to move into actual counseling. Finally! It's time to talk about why the client came to counseling in the first place and what they hope to gain from the experience. In this first session, you will begin to formulate your diagnosis. What is diagnosing? In the simplest terms diagnosing is putting a label on a set of symptoms that most accurately describes what the person is experiencing. Why do we diagnose? That's a very good question, and one that is a topic of hot debate among many practitioners. The main purpose of diagnosing is to make treatment across different members simple. The idea is that the person who completes the initial assessment can say Major Depressive Disorder, Single Episode, Mild, and anyone subsequent helping professional who works with that person can know exactly what is going on without completing a brand-new assessment. There are many practitioners across different disciplines (social workers, counselors, psychologists, psychiatrists, etc.) who feel that diagnosing is not helpful and actually is counterproductive because it puts a label on people and attempts to fit their own unique set of symptoms into a neat and tidy box.

If you are planning to be a counselor and work in mental health, you will likely have to diagnose the people who come to you for help. This is true in a community mental health setting or your own private practice.

If you offer counseling in a setting that does not require insurance (some faith-based counseling centers or private practices may take cash) you can avoid diagnosing, but at some point in your counseling career you are going to have to make that call. Diagnosing someone with a mental health condition is a huge responsibility. Their diagnosis will become a part of their medical record and can stick with that person their entire life. You have to take this VERY seriously; you cannot check out and just apply whatever diagnosis you would like to. If you ask a client whether or not they have ever seen or heard anything that other people can't see or hear (checking for psychotic symptoms), be prepared for a lot of them to say yes! Does this mean they are all psychotic? Probably not. A lot of people will report having a one-time, or maybe two-time, incident of seeing or hearing something that nobody else could. Your mind may start thinking about diagnosing them with a psychotic disorder such a Schizophrenia, but you need to be aware that most people have experienced a situation like that once or twice in their life. Most of the time it is just their mind playing tricks on them when they are in a heightened state, such as being very anxious or fearful. It could be Schizophrenia, but your precise and calculated questioning should lead you in the right direction. And remember, when you are diagnosing someone you are looking for a symptom set that is outside of the norm. You must consider what is normal for a person based on their culture, race, religion, etc. If it is a cultural norm for the person to

Are you feeling completely freaked out about the whole process of diagnosing yet? Let me help you relax. You have this awesome book called the Diagnostic and Statistical Manual of Mental Health Disorders (DSM) to help you out. The most current version (as of my writing this) is the DSM V, and this book includes the criteria for every mental health diagnosis there is. Remember that diagnosing is both an art and a science. The science is following the manual, writing down the exact symptoms observed/reported, and following the script of questions that should be asked. The portion of diagnosing that is an art is being able to have flexibility, change your course of questioning on the fly, and using discernment to understand what is really happening with this individual. Here are some tips to help you out!

Mental Status Exam

A mental status exam is an important part of the diagnostic process. Think of the mental status exam as being the mental health equivalent of a physical. When you go to the doctor they always take your height, weight, check your temperature, and ask various questions about your functioning to see how you are doing right then and there. You will not be checking vitals, but there are many things you are checking in a brief period of time. You need to be aware of your client's appearance, mood, speech, behavior, thought process, thought content, cognition, and judgement.

- **Appearance -** How does the person look? What is their posture, style of dress, their grooming, and emotional facial expression?
- **Mood -** Ask them what their mood is and document what they say. Look for congruence or discrepancies between their stated mood and the mood you observe.
- **Speech -** Are they speaking slowly? Quickly? What is their volume of speech? Their tone?
- **Behavior -** What are they doing? Did they sit? Stand? Are they making eye contact? Is their leg bouncing up and down? Are they wringing their hands? Is their behavior relaxed or anxious? Do you notice any tics or tremors?
- **Thought Process -** Do their thoughts flow logically? Are they connected? Do they shift quickly between topics? Are they fixated on a particular topic?
- **Thought Content -** What themes do you notice? Are they delusional? Paranoid? Depersonalizing?
- **Cognition -** Are they oriented? Do they know their name, the time, place, and what is happening?

- **Judgement and Insight -** Do they know they have an issue? Do they have a general understanding of cause and effect (do they recognize that choices have consequences)?

In the first session, you want to do a full mental status exam as part of (or before) your clinical interview. You need to be able to establish what the baseline of these areas is for your client so you can note discrepancies during future sessions. You want to do a brief mental status exam every time you see a client, even if it is just observational over the course of the session. Changes that you notice will clue you in to your client's functioning on that particular day, and discrepancies between what they say and how they present are excellent conversation starters.

SODFI

SODFI is an acronym that stands for Symptoms, Onset, Duration, Frequency, and Intensity. In order to get to the root of what is going on and give an accurate diagnosis you have to answer these questions.

Symptoms: What are the specific symptoms? Symptoms are basically the outward physical manifestation of what is going on internally. Many clients, when asked about their symptoms, will say something like "I have depression." an appropriate follow-up would be "what is depression like for you?" or "if I could see your depression, what would I be looking at?" or "tell me more about that." What you want to get to are specific symptoms, such as crying, sleeping/lack of sleep, loss of interest, mood swings, fits of rage, having little patience, etc. The more specific the symptoms the better.

Onset: Onset means when the symptoms began. This is very important as the onset of symptoms is sometimes triggered by an event. Whether or not there was a catalyst for the symptomology is important in determining the diagnosis as well as the direction of treatment. Unresolved trauma could be the underlying reason for why a person is continually experiencing anxiety, but simply treating anxious symptoms will only provide a short-term solution. The onset of symptoms has to be determined; even if the person says, "I've always been like this" that tells you something!

Duration: When the person is experiencing a symptom, how long does it last? 10 minutes? One hour? Days? Months? There are several diagnoses that require a specific symptoms duration to meet the diagnostic criteria, so you must ask about symptom duration.

Frequency: This question is similar to duration, but it is more focused on how often a symptom occurs. Does the symptom happen once every day? Once a month? Does it happen a specific time of day? Day of the week? Is there any correlation with the frequency of the symptom and another event? Understanding the frequency of a symptom gives more clarity to the underlying issue.

Intensity: This is just what it sounds like. How intense are the symptoms? Intensity of symptoms can be hard to quantify, but it's easier if you have the client put it on a scale of 1-10 (similar to what medical professionals do with pain). Find out when the symptoms are most intense and least intense to give yourself some context into what exacerbates or calms the issue. This will lead you closer to an accurate diagnosis.

It's not a problem if it's not a problem

Almost every diagnosis in the DSM has a note at the bottom that says something very interesting. It says "symptoms must cause significant impairment in one or more areas of functioning." Now this is one sentence down at the bottom so it is easily skimmed or passed over completely; however, this sentence has MAJOR implications for the person who is doing the diagnosing. As clinicians and people trained to look for and spot mental health conditions, we can go a little rogue sometimes. Yes, I have been guilty of this myself. I have spent a lot of time working in children's mental health and I cannot tell you how many children have come in with "Attention Deficit Hyperactivity Disorder-like symptoms." What am I talking about? Allow me to explain. A lot of kids are brought to therapy because there has been a major life change (family move, divorce, loss, etc.) and their parents/caregivers want to make sure they are okay. This is a great thing. The parents start talking about how little Johnny is very inattentive, he has trouble focusing on his homework, and doesn't sit still very long. All the bells and whistles in your head are going off right now shouting, "HE'S ADHD STUPID! DIAGNOSE HIM! DIAGNOSE HIM NOW!" But then you start asking some more questions. "How are Johnny's grades?" "They're fine", his parents respond. "Ok", you say. "Does his impulsivity and inattention get him in trouble at school or at home?" "No", his parents state. "It's just frustrating. I wish he could focus more." It turns out that Johnny's inattentive/impulsive symptoms are there, but they are NOT causing a significant impairment in one or more life activities. For Johnny, a diagnosis of ADHD would not be appropriate based on that little sentence at the bottom of each diagnosis criteria. The symptoms themselves are not enough for a diagnosis. There must be an accompanying impairment in life activities.

Speaking of working with children, you need to have a general understanding of child development and age-appropriate expectations. For instance, it is helpful to know that children tend to develop a sense of empathy (or caring for others) at around the age of five or so. It is unrealistic to expect a three-year-old to understand how his behaviors hurt another child's feelings. They just don't get it. Therefore, selfish behaviors from a child that age are developmentally appropriate. You might not like it and you might want to change it, but that doesn't make it pathology. What am I saying? Don't diagnose a three-year-old with Oppositional Defiant Disorder. When diagnosing, you are looking for behaviors that are *outside* of the norm for that age group/population.

Think horsies, not zebras
There's a saying that goes "when you hear hoof beats, think of horses not zebras." This phrase is generally used in the medical field but it applies to diagnosing mental health conditions as well. There are certain buzz words that clients say that make you think of one diagnosis or another. For example, when a client brings up mood swings you will likely begin to think

about Bipolar Disorder. It's typical to ask clients if they have ever seen or heard things that other people couldn't see or hear. Sometimes a client might respond with, "Sure. I've heard voices before." And you start thinking *GASP* Schizophrenia! If a parent states, "My kid is just defiant" you start thinking Oppositional Defiant Disorder! That kid has Oppositional Defiant Disorder! The hoofs are beating, and you are thinking zebras. Could a person with mood swings have Bipolar Disorder? You bet they can. But you also need to know that about 2.6 % of the population has Bipolar Disorder. It's not wrong to begin thinking about Bipolar Disorder for a client who describes mood swings, but you HAVE to ask a lot of questions and get at what's really going on. Schizophrenia? About 1 % of the population. And there are *a lot* of people out there who describe their own thoughts as "hearing voices", people who have thought they heard voices when they were alone in dead silence, and people of varying religions who truly believe they have heard the voice of God that no one else could hear. Do these people have Schizophrenia? Maybe, but probably not. You must ask the questions to find out. The hoof beats are getting closer, and you need to think "horses".

Your diagnosis for the client is *very* important. It's easy to get lazy over time after you have done hundreds of diagnoses and just start assigning labels as soon as you hear some buzz words.

Remember that, especially if you are dealing with insurance, your diagnosis is something that becomes part of the client's medical history. Diagnosing a fifteen-year-old with Schizophrenia might exclude him from being able to join the military at eighteen. The diagnosis you give can have far-reaching implications. If you come in half-assed, you could truly damage someone's future.

That being said, if a client meets a diagnostic criterion, then they meet it. You can't give a client a lesser diagnosis just because you don't want to diagnose Schizophrenia or Bipolar Disorder. You have to diagnose the person who is in front of you, but you also need to know what questions to ask and what factors to consider.

Practice Parsimony
The rule of parsimony implies that the simplest explanation is usually the correct answer. This goes right along with the prior hoof beats section (which ought to clue you in on just how important this is in diagnosing), except the focus of this section is the actual diagnosis you apply. A mental health diagnosis is meant to be fluid, and it can change throughout treatment as needed. If you are working with a client who meets the criteria for an adjustment disorder and you see them for several years working out the same issues, then they likely do not have an adjustment disorder but something deeper. As treatment progresses you will learn new things about the client, get new details regarding the symptoms, and gain a better understanding of how the client functions. This will give you a clearer picture of what the diagnosis should be and the appropriate means for treating your client.

Remember that a diagnosis can always be increased in its severity, but it can never be decreased. Once a client is diagnosed with something like Bipolar Disorder, there is no going back on the scale of mood disorders. Conduct Disorder is the most severe diagnosis for a kid who shows signs of negative acting out behaviors. Once you go Conduct Disorder, there is no scaling back to Disruptive Behavior Disorder or Oppositional Defiant Disorder. So, what does parsimony have to do with diagnosing mental health disorders? Use the least severe diagnosis to cover the greatest number of symptoms.

Exclusionary Factors
There are always, always, always potential mitigating factors when it comes to diagnosing. Was that clear enough? THERE ARE ALWAYS POTENTIAL MITIGATING FACTORS WHEN IT COMES TO DIAGNOSING. Your diagnosis needs to be accurate, and you must account for exclusionary factors when considering a diagnosis. The two most common factors in diagnosing are medical conditions and substance abuse. Why is this important? You might diagnose someone with something they do not have. Quick! What are the symptoms of hyperthyroidism? Change in appetite, difficulty sleeping (insomnia), fatigue, irritability, nervousness, changes in moods, and others.

Is it just me or did that sound a lot like depression? If a client sat in front of me and ran off a list of those symptoms the first thing I would think would be depression. I would ask more questions, but I would certainly be leaning that way. There are many medical conditions that can mimic mental health symptoms, and no, you don't have to memorize every symptom for every mental health condition - just be smart.

Always think "could this be something else?" and remember that it is always a good idea to suggest your clients have a check-up with their doctor just to be safe. Substance abuse is another HUGE mitigating factor in diagnosing. If a client sits in front of you and complains of intense paranoia, psychosis, violent mood swings, hallucinations, and an insane amount of energy you would probably be thinking about a diagnosis of a psychotic disorder or maybe Bipolar Disorder. A good question to ask a person who reports these issues might be, "Hey, have you used any cocaine lately?" You might want to phrase it differently, but those symptoms can be the direct result of a person abusing cocaine. This person might not have a psychotic disorder but a substance abuse disorder, because without the presence of the substance they are able to function normally. Now there is always the possibility that a person may not know about a medical condition or they might lie about substance use, but there is nothing you can do about those things. Ask good questions and make the best diagnosis you can.

Make sure to ask about the client's eating and sleeping habits. Why? Because those are two things we do every day, and it's easy to point to a change in those because they are consistent. Hypersomnia (over-sleeping) or insomnia (inability to sleep) can by symptoms of several mental health conditions, and are at the very least strong indications that something is up. The same can be said for excessive weight gain or loss. Always ask about these two things and you will have a good idea about how a person's daily functioning may or may not have changed.

Familiarize yourself with the DSM
You likely will never memorize the DSM in its entirety, because that's crazy talk. I mean, the thing is like 900 some-odd pages. Relax and don't try to

overdo it. What you need to do is focus on the most common diagnoses and become familiar with the symptoms in order to guide your questioning. So, if you see a person who begins by explaining sadness you may be thinking, "ok...this sounds like depression." Then they talk about being in a car wreck last year and how everything started going downhill from there. You ask them what they mean and the person states, "Well, now I can't even get near a car without becoming anxious and sad." There ought to be a thousand alarms ringing in your head at this point, pointing to potential Post Traumatic Stress Disorder. Here's the issue though: if you don't know what questions to ask, you cannot get at the symptoms you want. If you know; however, that PTSD is characterized by a traumatic event, recurrent and intrusive recollections of the event, recurrent distressing dreams of the event, efforts to avoid things that remind the person of the event, hypervigilance, increased anger, difficulty sleeping, etc. (not the entire diagnostic criteria; just portions) then you can ask the right questions for this situation. Familiarizing yourself with the DSM can be challenging, but it is something that will become easier throughout your career. You will see the same things over and over again and something will click. Don't freak out; you will get it.

CHAPTER 15

DIAGNOSTIC DANGERS

Little Boxes

When I read the DSM and took a master's level course in diagnosing (before I began work as a counselor) I began doing something that nearly all counseling students do. I assumed that the clients I saw would fit neatly into little tiny diagnostic boxes. I would chat with them and they would tell me their symptoms one by one, going down the list in order as it appeared in the DSM. Oh boy, was I wrong. Clients, for the most part, won't fit perfectly into one set of diagnostic criteria. Sure, you can check off a couple boxes here and there but it won't be easy. You might see a client who has depressive issues, relational problems, substance abuse issues, a history of trauma, attention/focus issues, anxiety, intense anger, and mood swings. As a diagnostician who wants to do right by my client, this is the stuff that keeps me up at night. What do you do? I don't really have an answer for you and I hate that. This truth is something that is going to plague you throughout your career as a counselor. We have tried (and it is a noble venture) to put objective parameters and labels on something that is subjective and nearly impossible to quantify. You could meet one hundred people who were diagnosed with Major Depressive Disorder, and while their symptoms may look similar, not a single one of them is exactly the same. Every single person you will ever see for counseling is a unique individual and it is a HUGE mistake to assume that they fit into a neat and tidy diagnostic box. The only answer I have is to treat each individual as just that - an individual. Sure, you have to assign a diagnosis if you are working with insurance and that's okay. Just use parsimony and try to treat what you believe to be the underlying issue.

Fundamental Attribution Error

When your job is to diagnose and your pay depends on you diagnosing, that's what you do. From the moment you lay eyes on your client you begin formulating a diagnosis. They share, you ask questions, and that diagnosis takes shape throughout your experience with the other person. This robotic laser-like focus on finding a diagnosis can have some unintended consequence though. As counselors, we are susceptible to what is known as the fundamental attribution error. Simply put, this is attributing every perceived negative behavior or symptom to pathology and ignoring all the other factors that may contribute to the current state the client is in. Many people who come to counseling do so as a last resort. They have been fighting and fighting a battle they just now have decided (or someone else decided for them) that they need expert help. The client who comes and sits in front of you is a human being, just like you. Their personality, attitude, and general disposition are all affected by external circumstances. They are not completely controlled by external factors, but they are certainly affected by them. Take this into account when doing a diagnostic evaluation. Has the person had a bad day? Did someone recently pass away? Is their mind preoccupied by more pressing issues such as health concerns or their financial status? Not everything you see, hear, and feel from a client is indicative of their internal personality or some pathology. A clinician only sees symptoms as pathology if those symptoms are outside of what is considered normal behavior. There could be an entire book devoted solely to the concept of "normal behavior", but it is vital to understand the cultural and personal implications of applying our own lens of what we consider to be "normal". Viktor Frankl once famously stated, "An abnormal reaction to an abnormal situation is normal behavior."

CHAPTER 16

TREATMENT PLANNING

Why do we diagnose? So we can competently treat. The point of diagnosing is to provide direction in treatment and supply any subsequent helping professional with a label so they know what they are dealing with. Most insurance companies require that a plan for treatment, or a treatment plan, be drafted and signed by the clinician and the client. The purpose of the treatment plan is to give clear and specific goals for treatment, as well as timelines for completing those goals. The treatment plan can also be thought of as a contract between the clinician and the client. This is another subject to which there is an entire graduate level course devoted, so you won't get all the information you need from here, but you will get the gist. If you work for an agency you will likely have to template for treatment plans, so don't sweat it. And if you are in private practice you are not on your own either. There is some great clinical software that will create insurance company friendly templates for you based on the data you enter.

A collaborative effort

A treatment plan, despite the belief of some, is not a document that the clinician creates in order to hold the client to certain standards. The goal is not to tell the client what they should be doing, but working with the client to develop a set of goals that are achievable and sustainable. Working together with a client on their treatment plan is key because it invites buy-in from the client. They are working for goals they want to achieve, not ones that you want for them. It is helpful to flat out ask your client, "What do you want to achieve in therapy?" That is a great starting point, and from there you can craft excellent goals.

Goals and objectives

A good treatment plan needs both goals and objectives. Goals are what the client wants to ultimately achieve and objectives are the specifics of how they will achieve those goals. Goals should fit into this criterion: they should be specific, achievable, and measurable. Here is an example of a bad goal: "John smith will be less anxious". That's bad. Here is a better goal: "John Smith will decrease the amount of panic attacks from five per week to two per week over the next three months as evidenced by self-report." That goal is better. It is specific about its measurement, it's achievable (notice we did not get rid of panic attacks entirely), and it is definitely measurable. Continuing with that same goal we can create some objectives for John. Usually you want at least two or three objectives per goal. Objective one: "John agrees to attend weekly counseling sessions and participate." Objective two: "John agrees to comply with his medication regimen set forth by his doctor". Objective three: "John agrees to learn and demonstrate an understanding of at least three coping skills for managing feelings of panic and anxiety." BOOM! That is a pretty solid set of objectives.

The language you use

A treatment plan needs to be written in a language your client can under-stand. If you are working with an elementary aged student don't set goals like this: "Joey Baloney will acclimate to his present environmental situation through the accumulation and sublimation of negative symptoms reducing the probability of achieving homeostasis." If you write treatment plans like that you are just showing off. You must use language your client can under-stand, but don't take it too far the other way either. There is such a thing as mental health counseling for three year olds, and your goals would not say, "wittle Johnny needs nappy nap after snacky snack." Find the balance between those extremes and you will be fine.

Begin with the end in mind

Never forget the overarching goal of therapy - to end therapy. You want your client to be free from their issues and not need you anymore, and that sentiment should be reflected in your treatment plan.

The functionality of symptoms

The human body is fascinating. It has the incredible ability to adapt to different situations and circumstances to keep us alive. Stop and think about it for a moment. Your body wants you to be fat. If you do the same workout every single day you will make some serious gains in the first few months, and suddenly those gains will stop. Your workout regimen that was so successful will no longer yield results. Why? Early on the exercise was new and your body had to use a lot of resources (recruit a lot of muscle) to move the weight around. But eventually your body will adapt and won't use as many muscles to move the same weight. It's the same when you start restricting calories. If you switch to a very low calorie diet you will lose some fat very quickly, but your body will catch on. It will go into starvation mode and start burning muscle instead of fat. Your body wants you to be fat, and no, it's not a cruel joke. It's evolutionary. You need fat. Fat keeps you warm and can sustain you longer than muscle can. You don't need muscle to survive as much as you need fat. And those are just a couple of examples of how amazing our bodies are at adapting to help us survive.

The same is true with our mind and our brain. Safety and survival are very important goals to our mind and we have the propensity to adapt in order to best survive in our environment. Anxiety and fear are evolutionary. They are there to keep us safe from danger, and they will do whatever it takes to do their job. If you were walking down the road one day and suddenly there was a rattlesnake right in front of you, you would probably freak out and jump backward. Your heart would be racing and you would be shaky. Why? Your mind has said "DANGER!" to the rest of your body and your body reacted by prompting you to jump backward and pumping adrenaline through your body so you could enter fight or flight to survive. That's great - we want that to happen! But how about a week later when we are walking down the same road and we have a similar reaction to a stick? Uh-oh. That's not such a great thing. You spotted the stick and your mind perceived it as a threat, prompting the same fight or flight response.

Do you see where I am going with this? Not all symptoms are bad, and we do not want to get rid of all of them. It's unhealthy to be stress-free, worry free, and/or never get angry about anything. You need your emotions and your body's physiological responses, but you need them to act appropriately. We don't want to get rid of the symptoms necessarily, but we do want to limit the negative effects and channel those symptoms into something positive.

When you think of ADHD, what do you picture? Most folks picture a child who won't sit still. They squirm in their seat, constantly move around, are fidgety, and generally bothersome to others. So, as clinicians, what would be our task in helping a child with ADHD? Many would say, "stop the fidgeting" and that seems like the obvious answer. After all, it is the constant moving around that people notice and that seems to get the child in trouble. It's a no-brainer, right? Well, not so much. There is some research that has been conducted that indicates that the fidgeting and moving are actually adaptive measures to help a person with ADHD. The physical restlessness might be associated with heightened mental control, which means - the squirming, moving, and general inability to sit still might be HELPFUL to a person with ADHD.

Why do you need to know this? Because many of the symptoms we see (and we would traditionally want to change) are adaptive measures a person has developed over a lifetime to help them. Changing these outside symptoms might not get to the root of the issue. Some symptoms can be seen as a positive if you look at it from a different angle.

CHAPTER 17

COUNSELING CLIENTS

Finally! I never knew that so much went into counseling before you started the counseling. In the next few sections we will dive into just that, the counseling. There are a lot of things that you should/should not do, and trying to memorize all of them will turn you into a mumbling ball of mush of the floor in the fetal position. Some of these skills you gain with experience, and some you bring with you into the session. All of them are important and they take practice. Like any skill, counseling is one that requires work and constant refining and reflection.

The Counselor Who Rarely Speaks
There are many skills you need in a counseling session that do not involve you saying a single word. This was one of the biggest revelations to me as a graduate student. When I thought of providing counseling to someone I thought of two things - talking and solving problems. Yeah, it turns out that one of those is done sparingly and the other one is not supposed to be done at all. Well, there went all my preconceived notions about being a counselor! Most of counseling is listening, and if you're talking I can guarantee you are not listening fully. And listening does not just mean using your ears. You have to pay attention to the entirety of what is going on around you. **Watch your client's body language.** A person's body language can reveal a lot about

what they are experiencing. Are sitting up straight and attentive? Are they slouching? Are they looking around the room? Are they biting their nails? Are they restless? Do their muscles tense when they are talking about a subject? Do they look away when you bring up something from their childhood? Holy cow that's a lot to watch for! But that's the job of a counselor - that's how you tune in to what's going on. A lot of times a client will say one thing, but their body language will betray them. I have sat with many clients who said that talking about their parents did not make them uncomfortable, only to watch them become fidgety and tight during those conversations. Listen to what they are saying - really listen.

As a counselor, you need to **listen for patterns.** A difficult skill to learn is how to distinguish between what is just minutia (trifling details) and what is important. Counseling sessions can be difficult because people generally like to talk...and talk...and talk. It's good that they talk; it is really good. Talking is part of the process and helps a person mentally work through what is going on. The problem is that once you open the spigot people tend to verbally vomit all over the place for a full hour. They typically do not know what the important pieces of information are (because they have come to you for help in deciphering that) and it all comes out...everywhere. Your job is to pick through the pieces and find patterns in their stories. Remember that listening for patterns is a skill, and any skill can be honed and improved with practice (that's what graduate programs are for). Sure, some people are naturally talented at things like this but don't beat yourself up if you don't get it right away. Skills take time to develop. Patterns are so important because they reveal pervasive issues or perceptions about the world. A client will (not purposefully) spill what the true problem is by explaining what the content problem is, over time of course.

I learned from my undergraduate education that there are three types of communication: verbal, nonverbal, and paraverbal. Verbal and nonverbal are easy, but what the crap is paraverbal? It sounds made up, doesn't it? Well, paraverbal communication is the messages that are sent through the tone, pitch, and pacing of our voices. Hearing what a person says is one thing, but understanding the paraverbal communication taking place is something entirely different. **Listen to your client's tone of voice, the volume of their voice, and their speech pacing.** Does your client speak more loudly or faster when discussing their family? Does their voice crack when discussing issues at work? What words do they emphasize? This last one is a biggie. A six-word sentence can have many different meanings based on which word is emphasized. Let's take a sentence like, "I didn't say you were stupid" and look at emphasizing different words. "I didn't **SAY** you were stupid" implies something entirely different than "I didn't say **YOU** were stupid" or "I didn't say you were **STUPID**". We have the same sentence here, but three different meanings. Words are very important, but the paraverbal communication that takes place can mean so much more.

In graduate school, you learn about a variety of different tools and techniques to get people to share about their issues and gain insight into what is really happening. Before I entered my graduate counseling program I never would have imagined that one of the greatest tools a counselor has is silence, shutting your mouth and just looking at someone. Why does this work? Because silence is awkward, and most people are very uncomfortable just staring at another human being for 50 minutes. The client will most likely keep spewing out details if you keep your trap shut and look at them.

When you do speak...
At some point during your session you will likely have to talk. It's *probably* going to happen. Don't get me wrong, there are some clients who make you feel like you spend an hour staring at them while nodding your head every once in a while. After the session those clients then say, "That was so helpful. Thank you!" And you are just standing there thinking, "What the hell just happened? How was that helpful?" Then there are clients who will flip the whole silence thing on you - they will just sit there and stare! Not cool people. Most clients will fall somewhere between those two extremes, and when it is time for you to talk you need to know what to say.

Use (their) metaphors - Don't do this right away, because that's weird. No one likes that guy who overuses metaphors. Pick your spots. Throughout the sessions you will be covering a lot of ground and talking about a lot of different things. During those conversations, your clients will inevitably use metaphors to describe certain feelings or situations. "Every time she comes close it feels like my heart is going to explode", "With the kids, the house, and my job I feel like there are a million pounds on top of me", "When I finally work up the courage to look for a new job I run right into a brick wall". These are just some examples of metaphors (yes, I know a couple of them are similes...nerds) that you might hear in a session. Roll with them! "It feels like your heart is going to explode? How do you defuse the bomb?", "A million pounds sounds like a very heavy weight brought on by a lot of things. What could we do today to take just one of those pounds off your shoulders?", "Brick walls are tough to knock down, but sometimes they can be climbed over." Use the metaphors (or similes) they do because they used them for a reason. This particular way of describing their situation makes sense to them and continuing the metaphor is often helpful in their problem-solving process.

Use encouragers - This seems silly in a vacuum. Using encouragers is a little strange at first and will feel odd for a while. Basically, using encouragers is exactly what it sounds like. You are encouraging the other person to continue talking and sharing. Bearing your soul and being emotionally vulnerable to someone who is basically a stranger is difficult, and using encouragers lets the other person know that you are not only listening but you also want them to continue. Encouragers can be both verbal and nonverbal. The most common of the nonverbal is nodding your head while the other person is speaking. Verbal encouragers include short words such as "okay" "yes" "I see" etc. You get the point. Encouragers show that you are invested in what the other person is saying and makes them more likely to continue.

Seek concreteness - Most of us use abstract terms or phrases in our everyday conversations - it's just part of the vernacular. We use vague generalities to describe situations, sometimes to keep them from becoming too real and sometimes just because we do not want to think about the situations any more than we have to. When a client is in a counseling session using vague terminology or phrasing, ask them to be more specific. Seeking concreteness, asking for more detail, or encouraging a client to further explain something is critical. An interaction between a therapist and a client might go like this: Therapist: "Tell me about your job" Client: "My job is tough, but it's what I do." Therapist: "Tell me more about 'tough'". That interaction concluded with the therapist seeking something more concrete, more specific, than just the abstract word "tough". Tough can have a lot of different meanings, and getting a better understanding of what the client's perception is will help you in the session. Plus, the client must dig a little deeper and think a little harder about their situation.

Paraphrase and summarize/reflect feeling - Knowing how to paraphrase and summarize are useful skills for any profession where you have to speak with people. Paraphrasing is repeating back a small portion of what someone is telling you to ensure that a) you are getting the facts the right and b) you are engaged in what they are telling you. Paraphrasing may look something like this - Client: "Yesterday I went to my mom's house and that jerk was there again. As soon as I pulled up in the drive-way he started in on me. I don't know what his problem is, but yesterday things seemed way worse." Therapist: "Okay, so you went to your mom's and things did not go well." That's it. Paraphrasing is taking what the client says and repeating a small portion of it back to them, except in your own words. Summarizing is similar to paraphrasing, but this is what you do with a larger narrative. You may paraphrase several times through-out a brief conversation, but summarizing would be saved for the end. Reflecting feeling is another useful technique that can be used easily with paraphrasing. Reflecting feeling lets the person know that not only are you listening, but you are understanding the emotions behind what is being said. Let's use the same example as before - Client: ""Yesterday I went to my mom's house and that jerk was there again. As soon as I pulled up in the driveway he started in on me. I don't know what his problem is, but yesterday things seemed way worse." Therapist: "Wow, you sound frustrated about what happened yesterday."

Provide insight - This skill is far more difficult than the previous ones mentioned. Paraphrasing and summarizing are the simplest, while reflecting feeling takes a little more practice. Gaining and providing insight requires you to go an extra step; you must understand what the client is saying, pull out the feeling, then make a larger statement about their situation that the client might not even realize themselves. Insight requires taking a little bit of a leap and trusting your gut. By the way, you will be wrong sometimes. And it sucks. You will attempt to make an insightful statement and your client will say, "No. It's not that at all." At that point you need to remain confident and continue. Insight, using the same example from before, may look like this - Client: ""Yesterday I went to my mom's house and that jerk was there again. As soon as I pulled up in the driveway he started in on me. I don't know what his problem is, but yesterday things seemed way worse." Therapist: "Correct me if I'm wrong on this, but you think this other guy is trying to take your father's place, and in your mind, he is not good enough." The client at that point might sit back and say, "Wow. You got it exactly right. I have never thought about it like that" or they might say, "Nope. No way. That is not what's going on here." Either way you went with your gut and took a shot. And no, being wrong on an insight does not make you a bad therapist, but being consistently wrong is not a good look. Pick your spots carefully on this, and gauge what insight you want to give per your therapeutic relationship. If you throw out a bombshell too early your client might feel a little embarrassed or defensive.

Say what you see (and hear) - during the session you will be attuned to your client; what they are saying, not saying, their tone of voice, how they are sitting, their facial expressions, and on and on. If you notice something, it's okay to bring it up. If you notice that the Jim Bob clinches his fists every time you mention his mother you might say, "Hey Jim Bob, I noticed that you seem to get a little tenser every time your mother is mentioned. Tell me about that." Or maybe Sally Sue has sat rigidly straight for three counseling sessions, but on the fourth she sits slumped and more relaxed. You might say, "Sally Sue, you seem different today; you look much more relaxed sitting there." It doesn't have to be a question, but the observation and discussion leads to introspection on the part of the client; introspection is good. They likely do not even know that they are having a response, and you pointing it out to a client can make them more in tune with their body and their emotions.

Reframe - Many clients are stuck, and the source of said stuckness is often faulty thought patterns. The act of simply challenging their perception of a situation by offering a different perspective can trigger magnificent effects. The adult client who endured childhood abuse may appear morose and lament being a victim. This is a great opportunity for you, the counselor, to look them directly in the eyes and say, "I don't see a victim in front of me. I see a survivor." You would then go on to point out the simple fact that they are alive, but also highlight positive steps they have taken. "Wow, not many people in your situation would have the courage to come to counseling. You somehow managed to get through all that, leave the situation, and graduate college? You are amazing." That simple turning of perspective is what we call reframing. Taking the same picture, a factual event that occurred, and putting a brand spanking new frame around it. Don't do this all the time and definitely do not do it when the client is first sharing their story - reframing too early or too much can come across as you denying the person their feelings or attempting to wash it all away with happy thoughts and good vibes. Let them tell their story, feel their story from their perspective, and then reframe down the road. Reframing also works exceptionally well with homework. Your clients will be setting goals and practicing new techniques to help them with their issues when they are not in session. When your client drags into the session and says, "Well, that thing you told me to do didn't work! Here's what happened..." Instead of lecturing them on what they did wrong or trying to come up with something new on the fly, you should reframe. Ask them, "What did you learn?" This question has far greater implications and requires more in-depth thought then, "Where did you mess up?" After all, the purpose of exercises and homework is to learn and grow, so that's a fair question. "What did you learn?" implies that even in perceived failure there can be victory. Reframing is powerful, and the smallest turn of phrase or perception can lead to big positive changes down the road.

Ask open ended questions - Asking open ended questions sounds like a no-brainer for a counselor, but it can be tricky. The problem is that in our everyday conversations we use closed ended questions all the time. "Do you want to get pizza?" "Did you order meat lovers?" "Are you going to finish that pizza?" "Can I take it?" "Did you just stab me with your fork?" These are the types of questions we ask (I love pizza), but as a counselor you need to ask open ended questions. Open ended questions invite long answers, conversation, a deeper thought. Let's say you are counseling Jack for severe test anxiety. You would probably want to know how long Jack has been dealing with this. The question that may pop into your head is, "Have you always had test anxiety?" That question invites a yes or no answer and requires little thought. A better question would be, "What happened the first time you noticed you had test anxiety?" This question requires a much longer response and a bit more introspection. From that question you will get details that you need to continue the session and learn what you need to know. Just remember this - if the answer to your question can be "yes" or "no", change the question!

Content vs. Process Counseling

Why do people come to counseling? Because of what they see, feel, and experience. They are seeing issues, feeling negatively, and experiencing something that does not jive with what they want to experience. What most clients don't know is that most of what they see, feel, and experience is what we call content; it's the surface stuff sitting on the exterior. The process, the underlying reason for the problem, is almost never addressed. That's why there are always new problems. Think of mental health issues being like weeds. Have you ever had to pull weeds? It can be grueling. And the worst part about it is that you can not just go around your yard quickly yanking up every weed you see. Why? You'll only get the stem. If you don't pull the right way with the right amount of force you will leave the root in the ground. And if the root is still in the ground you will see new weeds in a week. Now think about mental health problems again. Let's use an example. A man continuously fights with his wife because she wants to go out with her friends a couple of nights a week and he is not having any of that.

"I love her and I want her to have fun", he says. "I just don't think she needs to go out that often to do it." Surface (content) counseling will work with the man on communicating his feelings and being able express himself in a positive way. Process counseling (which can take some time) may reveal an underlying issue or deep-seated irrational thought. What if the man has abandonment issues? His mother left when he was a little boy and he was so crushed, so hurt by that experience that his psyche said "that is NEVER happening again." So, when a female that he loves dearly (his wife) wants to go out with friends his brain tells his body "you have to do something. Say something. Stop her from going - she might not come back!" That is the difference between content and process counseling. Please don't misunderstand me; the content is very important and needs to be addressed. However, we (as human beings) can get caught up in the content and never search for or address the actual process. If the man in our example learns how to only fix what he sees is the problem (getting mad at his wife and expressing that anger in a negative way), the root will still be there - and a new weed will pop up in a matter of weeks.

So, the million-dollar question (or in my case the $20,000 graduate school question) becomes "how do I get past the content and find the process?" I am going to give you some general guidelines here, but know that the specific skills needed to do this will be found in a graduate counseling (or related field) program. Here is the condensed version - you have to get in their shoes. Go ahead; I know feet are kinda gross and some people have awful smelling shoes, but you must get in there. You need to know how a client sees the world; this is called their schema. Their schema is something that they have spent their lifetime developing. It is how they take in information and make judgements about what is happening. It is literally how they perceive the world. Everybody's schema starts developing as a very young child and it changes throughout early childhood based on different experiences and reactions to those experiences. In order to better understand how a schema works (placing a value judgement on experiences), you need to understand just how memories work.

How memory really works

We often think of memories as files in a filing cabinet (or iPhone videos for you millennials) that we can look at and say, "Oh cool! That's exactly what happened!" This just isn't the case. **Memory is all about associations**. Every time we experience something, our brain processes that experience in its entirety. That means the smells, tastes, sights, sounds, touches, feelings, thoughts, ideas, etc. associated with that moment are all coded into our memory. Let's do a little experiment:

Imagine that you are at home and you picked up a big, juicy lemon. It's the brightest shade of yellow you have ever seen; a sharp contrast from the white cutting board. You lay it on a cutting board, grab your sharpest knife, and slice the lemon in half. As you slice it you see juice from the lemon ooze all over the cutting board as two or three seeds fall out. There is so much juice you can smell the sour. You slice the lemon into quarters, then pick a piece and take a huge bite out of it.

Are you salivating? Can you almost taste the sourness of the lemon? That's because you have tasted a lemon before, and just the thought of tasting another one brought back those memories. And...I just turned you into Pavlov's dog (if you don't know what that is, google it). Think about it this way. What comes to your mind when you hear a song that was popular when you were in high school? What do you think of when someone else is cooking a recipe your mom used to make? Have you ever caught a whiff of someone's perfume/cologne and immediately thought about a person you used to know who smelled like that? Remember that song that was playing during the worst day of your life? You hate that song...but why? Because you have made an association. Memories are not objective facts and things that happen just as they were - they have a slant to them, a bias. Your memories are shaded by how you were feeling that day, your perception of what was going on, and many other variables. Now let's get back to applying this to mental health. You need to ask your client about childhood memories. Ask them what they remember; the more details the better. Ask them what their earliest memory is, and then find out anything else they can recall. As they are sharing their memories, ask who was around them, what they saw, what they felt, and what they thought. The memories themselves may not be accurate and that doesn't matter because you are not concerned with specific facts. You are concerned with how the client *experienced* those moments and how those moments shaped their schema, turning them into the person they are today. This is how you get into a client's shoes. They remember what they remember because it was, and likely is, important to them. Recalling who was around them, what those people were doing, and how those people reacted to the situation will give you GREAT insight into how the client views how they fit into the world.

The facts don't matter (as much as you think they should)
One mistake counselors often make is getting bogged down in finding out facts. The actual events that happen are not really that important when you are counseling someone. I know that sounds a little crazy, but stick with me here. What matters is the client's *perception* of what happened. Their perception (how they take in and make judgements about external stimuli) determines whether or not they see an experience as a positive or a negative. Perception is what makes everyone different, and that's why it is really, really, really difficult to fit every client into a nice and neat theoretical little box to counsel them. One person who encounters a snake in their yard may experience that event as being traumatic and life-threatening, leading to the onset of Post Traumatic Stress Disorder (whether the snake was poisonous or even close to the person is irrelevant). Another individual may see the same snake at the same distance and think, "Oh cool! It's a snake! Maybe I should touch it!" Everyone is different and a mistake many counselors will make (I've done it) is using the argument "well the snake wasn't even poisonous so your life was never really in danger." **The facts are not nearly as important as the way the person experiences the event.** When you are counseling someone you must allow them to share the events and they saw, heard, felt, and experienced them. Their unique perspective on what happened defines their reality. Anais Nin once famously stated, "We don't see the world as it is, we see it as we are." Perception is more powerful than you think, and that's

mostly because you probably never stopped to think about it. Perception is what gives life context; it is what takes average and ordinary things and gives them meaning. I'll illustrate this simply. Let's say that I stood right in front of you, picked up the most precious photo you have, and ripped it to shreds. You would probably be upset with me, because well, what kind of a jerk would do such a thing? Let's say that I ripped up the same exact picture, only this time it was in front of a total stranger who had never met you or anyone in your life before. Would the stranger care? No. The act of ripping a picture has no innate value, but the value given to pictures through context (perception) is what matters to you. In the same way you cannot approach a therapy client and impose your own perception onto their life. You may say, "It's just a picture" but to them it is so much more than that.

Balance Gaining New Experience with Referring

Let's pretend - you have been working with an agency for over a year now and you receive a new client. That's no big deal because you have had many clients over the past year. When you look at the primary diagnosis you see something you have never seen before - Schizophrenia. You learned about Schizophrenia in school but you don't have any real experience in treating the disorder. Counselors are bound by ethics to treat within our boundary of competency, but we also have an obligation to service the clients we have as best as possible. Do you refer the client to someone else, or get your feet wet in working with Schizophrenia? Wow, this is a difficult scenario and the answer is not cut and dried. The correct answer will depend on the circumstances and what you plan to do if you continue working with the client. Does your supervisor have experience with Schizophrenia? Can you consult with a colleague on how to best treat the disorder? Or, do you have a colleague who specializes in psychotic disorders who could do better work for the client? The answers to these questions will help you determine the course of action to take. It is always good to gain new experience, and hell, even the greatest expert in any field was once new. That thirst and knowledge for new experience though has to be balanced with doing what is right for that particular client at that particular time.

CHAPTER 18

INTERVENTIONS

The interventions you use with your clients will be directly tied to your theoretical orientation. It's all based on your view of how the people tick, what makes it go wonky, and how to fix it. That being said, your theoretical inclinations and interventions based on other therapies are not mutually exclusive - that means do what you want to do! If you believe in Cognitive Behavioral Therapy you aren't only limited to those interventions. You can practice CBT and still put value in Freudian Projective Tasks or Existential Exercises. You can do whatever you want, but your interventions must have a purpose.

Talk Therapy - I tend to be a bit cynical by nature (it's something I'm working on), and I've heard what the cynics have to say about therapy. "So I get to pay someone about $100 a week to sit there for an hour and talk about my problems while they just nod their head and collect my check? How does talking about your problems make them better?" That's a fair question, and I believe it's a common sentiment. How DOES talking about your problems make them better? In his book, Pocket Guide to Interpersonal Neurobiology, Dr. Dan Siegel talks about a lot of things I am not smart enough to understand. However, Dr. Siegel is nice to enough to provide a layman's explanation in each of his chapters. Dr. Siegel states that our brains have two sides, a left and a right. The right side is where our emotions and intuition come from, while the left side is the logical and ordered side. Wellness comes from integration between the two sides, while dysregulation occurs when one side takes over and we become far too logical or far too emotional. The left side of the brain is not only logical and ordered, but it also houses our linguistic center. Talking about emotions and problems literally engages different portions of the brain, allowing a deeper level of processing than has been present before. Dr. Siegel states that brain scans have shown that the simple act of naming a feeling and saying it out loud can calm activity in the brain. That's how a person can sit and talk about their problems for an hour and feel much better afterward. Science!

Homework
Treat therapy like school; sort of. Do you know that different people have different learning styles? It's true - some learn better by hearing, some by seeing, and some by doing. Most people are not exclusive to one category and learn best with a little bit of a hodgepodge. Therapy needs to be managed and worked through in a way that can utilize those different learning styles - because after all, therapy should be a learning experience. Learning something is great, but if you don't apply that knowledge it can be wasted. That is why homework is necessary in therapy. Your clients need to try different interventions, see what works, review the results with you, and adjust accordingly.

Role play
Role play seems silly and it feels weird when you are first starting out, but you get used to it. Basically, you and the client pretend that the client is in a situation that causes them some sort of trouble. It might be interactions with family members, a boss, coworkers, etc. It feels weird and seems ridiculous, but it is great for preparing clients for possible outcomes of interactions. If you practice cognitive behavioral therapy you know how unhealthy and irrational thoughts can poison someone's disposition regarding a situation. Role play allows the client to safely endure a practice round of terrifying situations and come out the other safely, easing some of those negative thoughts.

Solution Focused Questioning

The specific and strategic questioning involved in Solution Focused Therapy are excellent tools. And by the way, you don't have to be a Solution Focused therapist to employ these techniques. I believe that these questions and the language of solutions work well and compliment just about any theoretical approach. You don't have to buy everything that Solution Focused Therapy is selling. Using the miracle question, scaling questions, coping questions, and exception questions is very helpful in moving clients toward wellness.

These are just a few basic and general interventions to use with clients. When you start digging into your particular theory and personal brand of counseling you will find interventions that work for you and interventions that don't. You aren't tied to any particular intervention or set of interventions, but (just like your theory) there will be ones that stick out to you and fit your personality and the personality of your individual clients.

CHAPTER 19

TERMINATING THERAPY

Do you remember what the goal of therapy is? The goal of therapy is to end therapy. Good therapy will, in theory, come to an end. In fact, discharge planning is something that should be done in the first one or two sessions. Why? Your eyes and your client's eyes need to be focused on the end goal. This is part of the treatment planning process. How will the client and/or the therapist know when treatment should be terminated? (By the way the word terminated has always sounded weird to me. It's the accepted vernacular for ending therapy so I get it, but it just sounds a little vicious or hostile. *In a bad Schwarzenegger accent* "Your therapy has been terminated". It just doesn't feel right. Oh well). Throughout the course of therapy the idea is that the client is learning; they are learning information about themselves they did not know, they are learning tools for managing difficulties in the future, and they are learning how to recognize future issues. The purpose of therapy is to end therapy. It makes sense that a therapist would want to hold on to a client (especially a good one) to continue helping them and working with them, but we must go back to those key ethical pillars. Is it in the client's best interest for them to come to therapy forever? No, because at that point you have moved from motivator to enabler. You run the risk of becoming a crutch or the focus of a client's transference. The truth is that you might not be there one day. If you (gulp) were to die, lose your license, move to a different state, quit the practice, etc. you won't be there for your client any more. If they are completely reliant on you, where does that leave them? You are trying to build personal resiliency and self-sufficiency. The purpose of therapy is to end therapy.

Planning for the end of treatment happens in the first or second session. The therapist and the client should begin the process with the end in mind. It is helpful to explain to a client the purpose of therapy, because they aren't thinking about the end. They have been dealing with an issue (typically for some time) and aren't in the mindset of expecting there to be an end. While you are treatment planning have a serious talk with the client about what the end of treatment will look like and how they can plan for it. The process of ending therapy should not be a surprise for the client. They shouldn't walk in one session and hear you say, "Well, today's our last session. Good luck out there!" Standard operating procedure is to give your client at least four weeks' notice before a planned termination of services; the key word there is planned. There will be times when clients will disappear, cancel services suddenly, or just flat out say "I'm only coming back for one more session." There's really nothing you can do in these situations, and there's obviously no ethical implications if the client decides to cancel therapy. If they ask for your opinion, tell them what you think is in their best interest.

CHAPTER 20

FEEL THE BURN

Ask anyone who has worked in the field of human services (counseling, social work, case management, etc.) what burnout is, and you will be able to tell from their face (before they even speak) that they have experienced it first-hand. If you do any job for long enough (not just social service) it becomes old hat and there are days when do not feel like going in and days when you probably feel like finding a new career altogether. The careers with the highest rates for burnout? In no particular order, they are doctor, social worker, nurse, teacher. Did you notice a commonality in that list? They all work with people. Working with people, especially people who are having trouble, can make your job stressful and difficult. So, how can we be proactive and limit burnout? Here are some tips:

1. Treat yo self - Unwind a little. Take some time off and have fun. When you aren't at work enjoy your family, friends, and do what you do to relax.
2. Leave your work at work - This one can be a little difficult depending on what your job is what the requirements of your job are. Some jobs might require you to be on call after hours or be available for emergencies by phone or in person. However, in most situations, you need to set some boundaries with your clients. Your clients need to know

what to do if they have an emergency (whatever protocol you have in place at your agency or in your practice, typically contacting 911) after hours. If you start returning phone calls, emails, or text messages after hours your clients will begin to assume that this is standard operating procedure for you. You don't have to be a jerk about it, but set limits. It is appropriate to tell your clients that you do not answer your phone or emails after hours and inform them of what to do if they have an emergency.

3. Have a support system - A support system is crucial. And your support system does not have to be just friends and family; you can lean on co-workers or other people in the field as well. When I was doing agency work (and really feeling the burn) one of the most therapeutic experiences for me was going to my graduate internship class and telling my classmates about all the junk. We would all take turns venting and sharing stories, and when we left we were refreshed and ready for the next week. Lean on your family, trust in your friends, and develop a system of other professionals who know what you are going through.

4. Let it out - I like writing, but I had no idea I liked writing until I started doing it. Allow me to explain a little bit. I knew from the moment I entered grad school that I wanted to move into private practice eventually. I also knew that I needed to build a brand and start marketing myself early. After a bunch of research, I found that a lot of people in the field became successful by writing a mental health blog and establishing themselves as an expert in their area through that medium. I didn't start writing because I wanted to write - I started writing as a marketing technique. Then something magical happened; I found my voice. I started writing, the words poured out of me, topics just came to me, and people told me they truly enjoy my writing style and what I had to say. When I ran into an issue, was frustrated with something in my job, or saw patterns that needed to break, I would write about it. The writing became cathartic for me. It allowed me to express myself, let my feelings

out, and share my ideas with others in a way that made me feel useful and appreciated. That is a textbook win/win. You don't have to write, but you need to find some way to let out the stress and all the thoughts that race through your head every day. You will be better off for it.

This work is not for everyone, and there is nothing wrong with that. Sometimes it takes getting into a job and feeling the burnout before you realize it, but don't stay miserable in a job you hate just because you have a degree in that field. If you are feeling the effects of burnout, find someone you can confide in and look at all your options. There are a lot of people who stick with it and things get better, but there are also a lot of people who find happiness in other career fields. No matter what you do, be yourself and stay genuine.

www.ingramcontent.com/pod-product-compliance
Lightning Source LLC
Chambersburg PA
CBHW030025290326
41934CB00005B/487